and June,
you find bits
!! Alastair
1/18

Empire Family

A hundred years of history –
1870 to 1970 – and a year or two beyond.

Alastair Forsyth

First published 2017

ISBN 978 1 9998700 6 5

Printed in Great Britain by
Biddles Books Limited, King's Lynn

Front cover: George Greensmith, my English Grandfather

To Jacki, for kindness and patience in letting me put together
these tales of a time long before our happy life together

Contents

1

Introduction

There comes a time when one has to try to make sense of it all.

I am not trying to track down the meaning of life. I agree with Isaiah Berlin, there is no such thing. We have to make of it what we can.

What I have set out to do is to tell the history of two families, the Forsyths who were Scots and the Greensmiths who were English, for the hundred years from 1870

I am 85 now. I am lucky that after 50 years I have finally had access to a great many of my grandfather's, my father's and my mother's and father's letters to each other and to their wider family and to their friends and business partners. This means I have been able to clothe with more detail the family story I have built up during my lifetime.

We don't write letters any more. But we were blessed to this extent. The family I am writing about, during the 100 years from the 1870s onward, were widely scattered. In the first world war the sons went off to France, Belgium, Holland, and Persia and Afghanistan, In the second world war they were separated, some in England and Scotland, others in Hong Kong, the Philippines, Germany, Sri Lanka and Australia.

Because they were, mostly, fond of each other, they wrote to each other regularly. It was before the age of e-mail and the letters they wrote, most of them by hand, were carefully kept. Most are letters received, only a few are letters sent; but in my grandfather Greensmith's case they are carbon copies of all the letters he sent, from 1917 onward. In addition he kept detailed notes of each of the cruises he went on, including his leisurely round the world cruise via Hong Kong, Japan, Los Angeles, New York, Cherbourg and home. He was interested in all he saw. A stockbroker not a seafaring man, he carefully noted the tonnage of each of the ships he sailed in.

My mother wrote always to her parents, from her schooldays onward. We have her father's replies but not her mother's. Her mother was at least as frequent a letter writer but tended to confine herself to domestic matters, rather than stray into business or politics. Her meticulous account book does however survive (first entry Harrods 1912).

The later letters between my mother and my father were written between them when they were separated in 1940 and in1941, in Hong Kong and Australia. They end with the last tragic days before the fall of Hong Kong.

Why am I writing all this? And who am I writing this for?

A first answer is that I am writing this for myself. I have been trying to square the legend – all that I have been told and all that I remember – with the archive – all the written material, the letters and postcards and other memorabilia that have lately come my way. I am happy to say that legend and archive diverge only to a small degree. Dates are more precise and the order of events is sometimes altered. But the family story remains largely the same.

The second answer is that I am writing for my family. I wanted them to have a true account of their family past, of who they were and how they lived their lives. It is also a moral tale. On the whole they were decent people, who set standards that their children and children's children could decently live by.

The third answer is that it is not a bad story. It has high points and low points, passes through times of war, times of peace, and times of change. I have put it all under the title of Empire Family, not because of any great contribution we made, but an Empire thread runs through it all, from the high point of Empire at the end of the nineteen hundreds, through imperial highs and lows, to the point we are now at, different from what we were, reasonably comfortable about our past and reasonably hopeful we can cope with the future.

Lizzie (my grandmother)
in Italy ?1907

2

1872 to 1914 – Greensmiths

My four grandparents were, on my mother's side, George and Lizzie Greensmith (Lizzie known in the family as Jack); and on my father's side, John and Mary Forsyth. The Greensmiths were English, the Forsyths were Scots.

The earliest Greensmith I know of is James Greensmith, born on 11th May 1809 in Nottingham. In the census lists his occupation is always given as blacksmith. He married Anne, from Langham in Rutland. Their first four children were born in nearby Melton Mowbray in Leicestershire – Mary (1838), William (1839), John (1840) and Emma (1841). After the move the next six children were all born in Whittlebury in Northamptonshire – Elizabeth in 1843, Henry (1845), Edward (1847), Sarah Jane (1850), Harriet (1851) and Emma (1854) (her sister Emma, born in 1841, died in 1851). The history of Whittlebury records the outbreak of cholera in the village in the latter part of 1854. It may have been cholera in that year that carried off these three.

Whittlebury in Northamptonshire was close to Wakefield Lodge, home of the Marquis of Southampton. James Greensmith, my great great grandfather, was his blacksmith. He probably left Melton Mowbray to take up the post. Arriving in 1841 or 1842, aged 31 or 32, he stayed in Whittlebury for the rest of his life. He was buried in Towcester, close to Whittlebury in 1872.

We do not know what became of Mary, their first child. The fourth child Emma died in 1851.

William, their second child became a footman, and later butler, at Wakefield Lodge.

John, their third child, my great grandfather, went South. We hear of him next in the household of Sir Francis and Lady Louise Goldsmid.

They were a distinguished Jewish family, settled in England since 1763. Sir Louis was the first Jewish barrister in England, the first QC in 1858, and subsequently in 1860 Member of Parliament for Reading.

Sir Isaac, father of Sir Francis, had entered the family firm of Mocatta and Goldsmid, bullion brokers to the Bank or England and the East India Company. In 1841 he was created the first Jewish baronet by the outgoing Melbourne administration. He made a large fortune from dealings in Portugal, Brazil and Turkey. He settled the Portuguese-Brazilian monetary dispute and was made Baron de Palmeira in 1846.

Complicating the nomenclature, Sir Isaac's daughter Rachel married Count Henri Salomon D'Avigdor, Duke of Aquaviva. Their grandson, Osmond Elim D'Avigdor- Goldsmid, in 1934 was created 1st Baron D'Avigdor-Goldsmid of Somerhill in the County of Kent. He is not to be confused with his great grandfather, Sir Isaac Goldsmid, created 1st Baron Goldsmid in 1841, almost a century earlier.

In 1849 Sir Isaac bought Somerhill, said to be after Knole the largest house in Kent. Sir Isaac died in 1859 and his eldest son Francis became the second Baronet Goldsmid. The house may then have passed to Frederick, younger brother of Sir Francis. Frederick however in 1865 became MP for Honiton in Devon (famous as the pot-walloper borough) and died in the following year. So he may never have lived there. Thus in 1866 Somerhill became the home of Sir Isaac's son Julian, younger brother of Sir Francis. Sir Francis died in 1878. Julian then became the 3rd (and last) Golsmid Baronet.

Both Sir Francis and Sir Julian played an important part in the life of the Greensmiths.

Sarah Varndell, later Sarah Greensmith, my great grandmother, was as a young girl a maidservant in Dogmersfield Park in Hampshire. This was the home of Lord Mildmay. Sarah came from Elvetham in Hampshire, not far from Dogmersfield. Her father it seems was a labourer on Lord Calthorpe's estate at Elvetham Park. She was later a maidservant in the household of Sir Francis and Lady Louise Goldsmid. It was there she met John Greensmith, a coachman in the same household. They married on 15th May 1869 in the parish church in Marylebone. Both are described as of "full age"- they were 28. Witnesses to the marriage were Anthony Adams and Fanny Varndell. James Greensmith, the blacksmith, is named as father of the groom and Daniel Varndell, carpenter, father of the bride.

The couple probably took up residence in London in 1869, the year when they were married. But we do not know when John and Sarah were first employed by the Goldsmids, or where they lived before they were married.

They may have lived in Somerhill before moving to the Goldsmid town house in Piccadilly.

Their first child Harry was born in 1870. However it appears from the 1871 census that John, aged 30, and Sarah were living at Hays Mews, close to the Goldsmids town house. But Harry was no longer with them.

My great aunt Alice, Harry's sister, told me that "through the good graces" of Lady Goldsmid, a place was found for Harry at "The Homes for Little Boys". The Homes were a chain of boarding schools for the sons of "the deserving poor", established in 1864 by a group of individuals including notably Robert Culling Hanbury, MP for Middlesex.

The first "Homes for little Boys" London site became overcrowded and a new site was purchased on the South Downs, near Farningham in Kent. When complete, the establishment comprised 11 cottages, each for 30 boys, with living-in house parents. The boys were trained for apprenticeships,. It was a revolutionary concept at the time, formally opened by Albert, Prince of Wales in 1867. It survived into different times and eventually in 1952 was handed over to the state.

According to Aunt Alice Harry went to the Edgeware branch and died there, she thought, at the age of about ten of diphtheria. However I have a note stating that Harry died in March 1882 aged 11 years and 7 months and was interred at Whitby church, Stanmore in Middlesex. This confirms he went to one of the earlier "Homes" in London, and not to the newer Kentish site.

The sending away would be thought unusual today, but it cannot have been practical for the Greensmith parents to care for an infant child and stay on as coachman and maidservant in the Goldsmid household in London. Placing their child in a home may have been the only (unhappy) solution.

George Greensmith, my grandfather, their second child, arrived in 1872, two years after Harry. According to my mother he was born in a mews house in Hay Hill, Mayfair, above a stable. Alice, his sister and my great aunt, followed in 1873.

In the meantime, in 1871 Charles Voysey came to live in London. He had been an Anglican priest in Yorkshire but was expelled for "heterodox teaching". He did not believe in the divinity of Christ nor in the doctrine of eternal punishment. He went on to found the Theistic Church in Swallow Street, Picadilly, and held services in St George's Hall, Langham Place. John Greensmith followed Charles Voysey into the wilderness, to the horror of his

Methodist parents. His three children, Harry, George and Alice, were the first three children to be baptised by Voysey.

Voysey lived on until 1912. His son was the well-known English architect of the same name.

It may well be that it suited Harry's parents to place him with a secular institution, given that their employers were Jewish and they (possibly both of them) were " heterodox", ex Methodist and now Theist.

But tragedy struck twice. John fell ill and returned to his father's birthplace, Nottingham, to be cared for. He died in 1875, aged only 35, leaving Sarah a widow, with three young children, George aged 3, Alice aged 2 and Harry (in the home) aged 5.

How did Sarah survive? It seems John's brother, William, former footman, was very good to the family. Aunt Alice says he was a Christadelphian. And John's sister, or wife, Aunt Fanny, "whom they all liked", stood by them.

However, help from the Goldsmids was crucial. When Sarah moved to the house in Gerard Road in Chelsea, where she lived for the rest of her life, Lady Louise stood surety for payment of the rent. Sarah's lodgers provided her income.

Three years later in May 1878 Sir Francis their employer also died. He collapsed at Waterloo Station. The Times (on 4th May) reported the event. He was succeeded, as third baronet, by his younger brother Julian.

We know little of these years but it seems the Goldsmids, that is, Sir Julian, after the death of Sir Francis, looked after Sarah and the children, securing for Sarah her lodging house in Chelsea and sending George and Alice to school.

Alice remembered their visits at Christmas time to the magnificent Goldsmid mansion in Picadilly, to report on their progress. She remembered waiting in the hall, among the liveried footmen, and how George made her laugh. Later, she said, when he was rich he dined with the Goldsmids.

We do not know which school the two children attended. It may have been one of the secular schools founded at the time by private benefactors. Nor do we know how they performed. The family story is that George's first job on leaving school was as a clerk in the British Museum, a job the Goldsmids might have helped him to obtain. It is said that his family was greatly upset (because of the loss of a steady income?) when he left the museum job to join a stockbroker's office. But George in 1892 was 20 and the 1890s were a boom time in the City of London. George would not have been immune to the attractions of earning elsewhere far more than the British Museum was ever likely to pay .

In 1896, both aged 29, George and Lizzie Vine were married. Lizzie was a Londoner although her family came from Wisborough Green in Sussex. Her father was a decorator and with him she visited many of the great houses of London. But the rich did not pay their bills and the business failed. She was petite and pretty as a young girl and I was told a portrait of her reached the Royal Academy.

More important, she was a merry, warm-hearted wife, mother and grandmother.

She walked a lot in Chelsea, always stopping to tip a Chelsea Pensioner. In her astrakhan coat and hat she walked me to school from Sloane Square to Victoria Station. She is remembered for her sayings: "If horses knew their strength they would rule the world"; "The wardrobe is the biggest domestic killer". She sang: "Pretty little Polly Perkins of Paddington Green"; "Goodbye Dolly Gray" and other Boer War numbers. She told riddles;

"A little red man in a little red coat, a stick in his hand and a stone in his throat, if you tell me his name I'll give you a groat" A cherry of course.

—

In 1897, a year after they were married, my uncle, Reginald Eustace Greensmith, was born, followed six years later, in 1904, by Marie Elaine Greensmith, my mother.

It will be noticed the names were not traditionally English. These were the years of the Entente Cordiale, when everything French was fashionable. My mother always remembered her beautiful French dolls.

In 1906 George and Lizzie gave a sedate party at their new- built home, "Weybourne", in Woking. The gentlemen were in formal wear and the ladies in long dresses and bonnets. My mother, two years old, wore a frilly dress with a bonnet to suit. Nanny was in attendance, and on guard while my mother toddled about among the guests.

Next year, according to a light-hearted piece in The Rialto (a stock market news sheet, December 18 2007) George joined Bourke, Cuthbertson and Co and stayed with them when "they retired from business to make room for the new firm, Bourke, Schiff and Co"

The Hon. Harry Bourke in this piece says he "first became a member of the London stock Exchange in 1864, and I have had enough of it. The good old days are no more, and cutthroat competition with mushroom competitors pleaseth me not. Happily I have not to apply to the Stock Exchange Benevolent Society for an old age pension. I am as comfortably off as I look and love my Derbyshire home, close by the dear old River Dove where a fly fisherman can fly- fish to his heart's content"

I am not sure I would necessarily warm to him. He goes on to commend his other partners who are staying with the new firm, among them Mr Moritz Otto Schiff "who comes from Frankfort on the Maine – and (pardon the joke) always has an eye to the main(e) chance. Ha, ha! But as an Irishman let me add there is nothing "main" about him. Ha, ha, ha!"

This all sounds like good Stock Exchange ribaldry. Harry Bourke was indeed an Irishman, related to the Earl of Mayo, a Viceroy of India who was notoriously murdered by one of the convicts while on a viceregal visit to a penal colony in the Andaman Islands in 1872.

The Otto Schiff referred to may not have been tremendously amused by Harry Bourke's endorsement. He was a junior member of the Schiff family of New York. Jacob Schiff, the senior member, died in 1920 leaving an estate of US$35 million. The connection proved invaluable later, ensuring Bourke Schiff's survival.

Lastly in the list of partners whom Harry Bourke commended is George Greensmith "and when I remind you that he came to us from Paul Nelke I need not tell you that he knows his way about."

Who was Paul Nelke? His family archive is with Southampton University. The Vanity Fair cartoon shows him in a financier's top hat and successfully plump. It is not a name linked in any way to George Greensmith in family lore.

However there is an oddity about Hon. Harry Bourke. The piece in The Rialto depicts him as leaving the firm in 1907 for a fly-fishing retirement in Derbyshire. In Jane Ridley's Life of Edward V11 she tells of Edward's visit to Marienbad in 1897. "In the afternoons the prince took damp drives through the thickly wooded hillsides with a new friend: Mrs Eddy Bourke".

"Emma (Bourke), in her early forties, was manipulative, with a history of sending poison-pen letters. Her husband, who was twenty years older than she, was a son of Lord Mayo … though a stockbroker he was often short of money."

"To his old mistresses Bertie was unfailingly generous. Emma Bourke appealed to him when the 1907 City panic caused financial ruin to her husband's firm. "Mon Roi", she wrote, "my husband's capital has all been swept away and here we are, he at 72 and a very sick man, left without anything. Would you", she implored, "for the sake of a friend in distress, use all your influence with Sir Ernest Cassel to help us all he can?" Bertie forwarded Emma's letter to Cassel. "It would be more than kind of you if you could be induced to give them a helping hand." Two months later Eddie Bourke was dead. Within a year Emma had become engaged to her old flame, Lord Clarendon.

Harry and Eddie were not the same person, they were brothers. What happened in 1907? Did Bourke Cuthbertson collapse? Did George and other partners see it coming and take evasive action? Was the article in the Rialto a Stock Exchange joke, covering up a calamity?

Bourke Schiff however survived and prospered.

In 1908 the Greensmiths went on holiday to Madeira. Reid's Hotel was amply photographed and is probably where they stayed. George on a rather skinny mount, with his camera strung on his shoulder, looks a less than confident rider.

After Madeira comes a trip to the Italian lakes and to Milan, but no names or dates or subtitles. The delightful pictures we have of George and Lizzie, (George in a Homburg hat, Lizzie in a flower-decked bonnet) were taken of them at a café table beside the water. The camera case prominent on the table we still have.

Madeira was not the Greensmiths' first foreign trip. This was their visit to the tulip fields of Holland. The date is unknown but it made a lasting impression. Kitty and Catherine, later their long serving Sloane street maid and cook, gave Lizzie each Christmas a "Dutch interior" calendar for a prominent fireside place in the drawing room.

In 1909 George bought "a new 1909 type 14/20 Renault chassis fitted with fashionable new Three Quarter Landaulette body". It cost £685 including one guinea for painting the initials GG on the door rails. The earlier car was a Panhard. The extra for a coat of arms was not included. Wibberly was the chauffeur.

Aged thirteen in 1910 Reggie would have left home for Charterhouse.

War broke out in August 1914. Reggie at the time was in Compiegne and had to hasten back. George aged 42 joined a volunteer unit for home defence. Reggie tried to join up but was rejected as too young. He joined his father instead in the volunteers.

18 in 1915 Reggie applied again and was accepted. He was directed to join HMS President on 5 September 1915 with the rank of probationary sub-lieutenant in the Royal Naval Air Service. This was the beginning of his war.

George's second car, the Renault

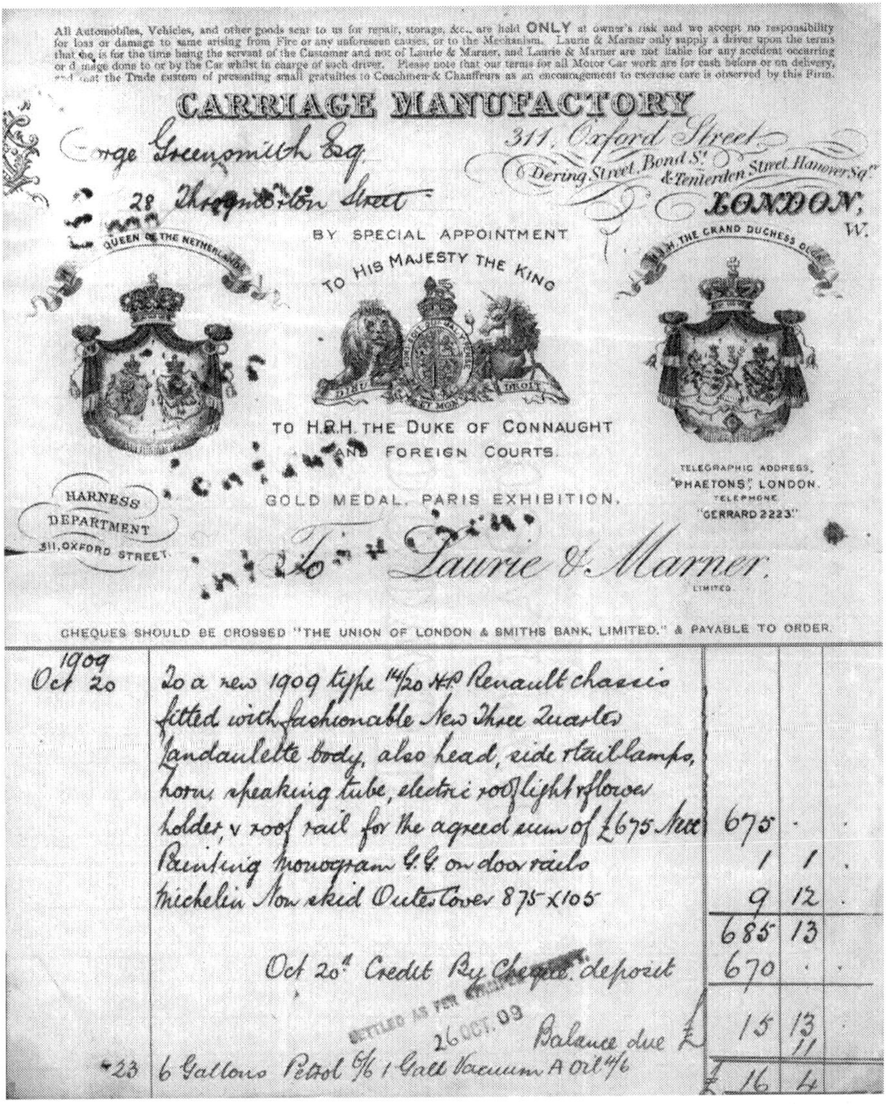
All Automobiles, Vehicles, and other goods sent to us for repair, storage, &c., are held ONLY at owner's risk and we accept no responsibility for loss or damage to same arising from Fire or any unforeseen causes, or to the Mechanism. Laurie & Marner only supply a driver upon the terms that he is for the time being the servant of the Customer and not of Laurie & Marner, and Laurie & Marner are not liable for any accident occurring or damage done to or by the Car whilst in charge of such driver. Please note that our terms for all Motor Car work are for cash before or on delivery, and that the Trade custom of presenting small gratuities to Coachmen & Chauffeurs as an encouragement to exercise care is observed by this Firm.

CARRIAGE MANUFACTORY

311, Oxford Street
6 Dering Street, Bond St. & Tenterden Street, Hanover Sq.
LONDON, W.

George Greensmith Esq
28 Throgmorton Street

BY SPECIAL APPOINTMENT
TO HIS MAJESTY THE KING
QUEEN OF THE NETHERLANDS
H.R.H. THE GRAND DUCHESS
TO H.R.H. THE DUKE OF CONNAUGHT AND FOREIGN COURTS.
GOLD MEDAL, PARIS EXHIBITION.

HARNESS DEPARTMENT 311, OXFORD STREET

TELEGRAPHIC ADDRESS, "PHAETONS," LONDON.
TELEPHONE "GERRARD 2223."

To Laurie & Marner.
LIMITED.

CHEQUES SHOULD BE CROSSED "THE UNION OF LONDON & SMITHS BANK, LIMITED." & PAYABLE TO ORDER.

1909 Oct 20	To a new 1909 type 14/20 H.P. Renault chassis fitted with fashionable New Three Quarter Landaulette body, also head, side & tail lamps, horn, speaking tube, electric roof light & flower holder, & roof rail for the agreed sum of £675 Nett	675	.	
	Painting monogram G.G. on door rails	1	1	.
	Michelin Non skid Outer Cover 875 x 105	9	12	.
		685	13	
	Oct 20th Credit By Cheque deposit	670	.	.
	SETTLED AS PER CHEQUE 26 OCT. 09 Balance due £	15	13	
23	6 Gallons Petrol 6/6 1 Gall Vacuum A Oil 4/6		11	
		£ 16	4	

The invoice

3

1872 to 1914 – Forsyths

On the Forsyth side we cannot climb very far up the ancestral tree

The first Forsyth I know anything about is my great grandfather. He is the first of our Forsyths of whom some personal memories remain. He was Arthur Lachlan Forsyth. On 3rd October 1854 he married Agnes Evans. They were both 32, both born in 1822. At the time, according to the Montrose Parochial Register, Arthur was a railway guard.

Arthur was "with the railway" all his life. The railway was I think the old Caledonian Railway, subsequently incorporated in the L.M.S, the "London Midland and Scottish".

Arthur's married life was less straightforward.

There was a first marriage before his marriage to Agnes. Arthur, aged 24, married Isabel Craig on 5th June 1846. They married in Brechin, Isabel's home town, not far from Montrose. He is described on the marriage certificate as a flax dresser. Arthur and Isabel had a daughter called Catherine. We hear no more of wife Isabel. She may have died, possibly in childbirth; but the record of deaths only begins in 1855.

Agnes before she married Arthur also had a daughter. The father according to the Montrose Parochial Register was Charles Walker. The daughter, born on 29th March 1845, was baptized and named Jane Evans Walker. Charles and Agnes were unmarried. Agnes was 23. Jane Walker never seems to have lived with her mother. At the age of 35 she married John Tevendale, a farmer, and lived on until 1921.

In 1854 when Agnes married Arthur he was living in Erskine Street, Montrose. Agnes' address was North Links, Montrose.

On 17th August 1855, eleven months after the marriage to Agnes, a son was born, but the mother was not Agnes. It was a domestic servant called

Jessie Henderson. It was Jessie's son who was my grandfather. The entry in the Register of Births names him as illegitimate but baptized, and named John.

The tale we as children were told was that Arthur, no longer a young man, married a young lady who was pregnant with a child that was not his own. He nevertheless gave the child his own name, thus saving him from the stigma of illegitimacy. In other words it was a selfless and noble act.

I realized later that if this was the case none of John's descendants were properly Forsyths. This was a bit of a blow. I wrote to my father's cousin Charlie Allan to ask the name of John's real mother. He said he was unable to help.

My sister-in-law Marie established what I believe to be the truth – that John and the rest of us were all Forsyths, but that John technically, in the eyes of the Church of Scotland, was illegitimate, not being born to married parents. According to my Aunt Nan, Uncle Allan's wife, the men of the family, including Charlie Allan it seems, were always shielded from this dreadful truth but the women always knew.

So it seems Arthur, aged 33, was not a generous protector of a poor forsaken girl: Jessie was a servant girl, possibly a servant in his own house, made pregnant by him after he married Agnes.

Agnes was one of a prolific family in the nearby town of Laurencekirk. It was there my grandfather John was born. In other words it seems that the recently re-married Arthur behaved disgracefully, but that Agnes, surprisingly, remained true.

Catherine Forsyth, daughter of Arthur's first marriage, continued to live with Arthur and Agnes, his second wife..

Five years after grandfather John was born, Arthur and Agnes in 1860 had their own son, whom they named Arthur. Before that, in 1856, they had a daughter, Eliza. They went on to have two more children, Matilda in 1863 and Elizabeth in 1865.

In Grassic Gibbon's novel, Sunset Song, all about this part of Scotland, the farmer's wife pleads "No more bairns!" The husband replies "The Lord bade us go out and multiply. Who am I to stand in the way of the Lord?" There was no stopping them. In the novel when twins came the wife killed herself.

Arthur at some stage moved to Clocksbriggs. This is in charming countryside but too small a place to feature on any map I have come across. Google locates it three miles East of Forfar along the road to the seaport of Montrose, seven miles further on.

The birth certificate of Arthur's youngest daughter Elizabeth, states she was born on the 27th September 1865 at Clocksbriggs, and that her father's occupation at the time was "stationmaster". At least he had progressed from flax dressing, an understandable switch given that the railways were booming. He was 43. In 1854 when Arthur and Agnes were married he was a railway guard. Eleven years later he had progressed to station master.

The station house at Clocksbriggs was pointed out to me by my aunt the first time I passed by. It is a lone house in a shallow green valley and at that time appeared to be little more than a hen coop. Clearly Clocksbriggs was not a station of great importance.

A "Parly train" ran daily along the railway line. It was so-called because Parliament had decreed that to retain the right to use the line at least one train had to pass through daily. It did not need to be full.

One of the tales told about Arthur was that as station master (at Clocksbriggs or later at Forfar?) he walked along the platform calling out "all change here for (then a long list of names)". When he was told it was a cattle train he walked back down the platform calling out "keep your seats gentlemen". The impression I received was that he was thought to be eccentric, or possibly not very bright.

One of Arthur's rare appearances in the press was in a report in the Montrose, Arbroath and Brechin Review of 13 December 1867 on proceedings in the Sheriff Criminal Court.

"John Ferguson jun. Woodside of Kinnell", it says, "was charged with having assaulted to the effusion of blood Arthur Forsyth, a railway station agent at Clockbriggs station, and by striking with clenched fist Agnes Evans, or Forsyth, who interfered to stop him assaulting her husband. He was sentenced to pay a fine of £5 or suffer 10 days imprisonment". Arthur was 45 at the time and the marriage was clearly on a firm footing.

It was as station master at Forfar that Arthur ended his time with the railways. This was a town only three miles away down the line from Clockbriggs. He lived there at the station master's house.

My Aunt Nan told me that when he retired he moved back to Clockbriggs, to a cottage up the hill above the station. Arthur and Agnes both died aged

87 in 1909. According to the record they were resident at the time at Hillock Cottage, Clocksbriggs. They were 55 years together.

Very recently there was a cottage for sale, advertised as Station House, Clocksbriggs. It was offered at £120,000 and sold. In the prospectus it is described as "a nineteenth century cottage, being a former British Rail property". Perhaps this was the home he retired to, rather than the hen coop? I wonder if the present owners have deeds and can trace the ownership back?

I know more about John than about his father, although not much. In 1887 when he was 32 he married Mary Heiton Allan of Kinnaber. She was daughter of James Allan, a miller. Elizabeth, maiden name Lowe, residing at Darnick,near Melrose in the Scottish Borders, was her mother, She was known as Bessie.

Bessie Lowe's grandmother was Mrs Elizabeth Fisher or Heiton. According to a legal document of 15th February 1860, providing for the distribution of assets as between James and Elizabeth in the event of the pre-decease of either, Elizabeth was entitled to a fourth share of her deceased grandmother's estate. The Heiton family owned Darnick Tower for 600 years. It was offered for sale for the first time in 2015 by the present owner, Fionne Heiton (or Fisher), who now lives in New Zealand.

It is clear from this that Mary Heiton Allan and her children are descendants of the Darnick Heiton family.

John's usual residence at the time of his marriage in 1887 was 27 Balmain Street, Montrose. At some time John and Mary moved to River Street, close to the little port in Montrose, which now mainly serves the offshore drilling rigs. It was there that my father was born, in 1897.

River Street smelt of fish and the sea. In one of the warehouses there was a tank in which a seal was kept. I remember as a small boy being taken to see it. Somewhere too I have seen a picture of John Forsyth, in the street outside a warehouse, standing proudly by a steam engine. I assume it was his and used for hauling coal.

Later on the family moved away from River Street, to Panmure Cottage, known in the family as "Pancot". This was a newly built modest Victorian villa, over the road from the green-domed Montrose Academy, where all the children went to school. The letterhead was 8 Panmure Place, the telegraphic address "Forsyth, Dock" and the telephone number 5A

When we stayed in "Pancot" in the 1940s, after my mother returned from Australia, the swords, uniforms with First War stripes of rank, and Sam Brown belts were still there in the attic, slung from the rafters. Stacked with them were manuals for the use of the Lewis Gun.

The Forsyths of Montrose may have been better off than the Allans of Kinnaber but the difference was not great. When the Allans, country dwellers, went to tea with the Forsyths, town dwellers, the Allan cousins, according to Charlie Allan, were always admonished: "cannie wi' the butter!"

Kinnaber, the Allan's ancestral home, is a hamlet, a little way inland from Montrose. It has a pleasant water meadow and an old mill, converted in wartime to an electrical generator. Mary's father was the miller and the family lived in the mill house. Charlie Allan, my father's cousin, took me there once, long after the mill had ceased working. The buildings had been fenced off so we could not get near, but looked down on them from the roadside. He showed me where the front room was. At the end of a cold raw day he said the farmers would come in and sit on benches round the wall. Old father Allan would pour a dram as each of them came in. Nothing was said at first - maybe just a comment on the cold. Slowly they thawed.

The "Scots Quair" novels (of which Sunset Song is one) have the flavour of those times, the hard lives on the land, raw weather and little money.

Darnick Tower, Melrose

My Scottish grandmother was called Mary Heiton Forsyth. Her maiden name was Allan. She was one of the Allans of Kinnaber in the County of Angus.

I asked about the Heiton name and was told it had something to do with the Scottish borders and assumed it was no more than a place name. However when my father wrote in 1931 to ask George and Lizzie Greensmith for their daughter's hand in marriage he describes his mother as coming from "good Angus and border families".

After the London wedding, my mother and father went on honeymoon to "Peebles Hotel Hydro (telephone no 2)" "still rated the leading hotel in the Scottish Borders".

They visited Melrose Abbey nearby on October 21st 1931 and also "Dalnick Tower", according to my mother "an old 14th century keep. It is a show place and belongs to some distant connection of Rusty's mother and so we stayed quite a time".

I paid no further attention to Darnick until I came across a legal document subscribed on the 15th February 1860 between James Allan, miller, residing at Kinnaber Mills near Montrose, on the one part and Miss Elizabeth Lowe, residing at Darnick near Melrose, of the other part.

In this document it is specified "that the said Elizabeth Lowe has right to one fourth of the estate of the deceased Mrs Elizabeth Fisher or Heiton her grandmother. James Allan (1825 – 1808) married Elizabeth "Bessie" Lowe in 1860. Their second child was Mary Heiton Allan.

So Bessie Lowe was Mary Heiton Forsyth's grandmother, and my grandmother's grandmother. In turn Bessie's grandmother was a Heiton and left to her a quarter of her property, Darnick Tower

My mother was right: it was a distant, but meaningful, connection.

The Tower had been in the possession of the Heitons for 600 years since it was granted to them by King James IV of Scotland. Sir Walter Scott who lived nearby wanted to buy the tower but his old friend John Heiton refused to sell. It subsequently descended from generation to generation. It was offered for sale for the first time in October 2015 by the present owner, Fionne. She is married to a Nepalese and they live in New Zealand. Her intention was to donate the proceeds of the sale to her Nepalese earthquake charity, First Steps Himalaya, aimed at providing early years help to Nepalese children. I asked if they might be interested in leasing the property but the estate agent said they were not.

The Tower is Grade A listed. The oak door is reputedly from Mary of Guise palace in Edinburgh. It was originaly built in 1425 after a grant of land to the Heiton family from James the First. The last great clan battle took place there in 1525, between Scott of Buccleugh and the Earl of Angus. It was witnessed by the young James Vth. In 1545 it was attacked by the English army. A new charter was granted by Mary Queen of Scots to Andrew Heiton in 15 60 (1566?) Walter Scott was a frequent visitor and wanted to buy the tower but his friend John Heiton refused to sell. Juliet Heiton was born in 1904 (same year as my mother). She was a flight Sergeant with the RAF in the war.

Subsequently she bred Himalayan wild goats. She had no children and when she died in 2002 she said she would like the "wee lass to have the tower". Fionne inherited when she was 15. She and her Nepalese partner now live in New Zealand and have 12 year old twins.

The Loss of the Falklandbank 1907/8

The Andrew Weir & Co. sailing ship Falklandbank, 1,913grt, was built by Mackie & Thompson, Glasgow, in 1894; she disappeared at sea in December, 1907, having sailed the previous month from Port Talbot for Valparaiso with a cargo of coal.

My Scottish grandfather John Forsyth obtained for his second son Arthur a place on board to "Falkland Bank", a sailing ship, bound for Valparaiso in Chile with a cargo of South Welsh coal. It set sail on 9th November 1907 from Port Talbot. It arrived in Montevideo in Uruguay on 27 December 1907. It was last "spoken to" close to the Falkland Islands. Neither ship nor crew were ever seen again.

Copied from a worn press cutting Nov 13 2014:

Glasgow ship given up for lost

Montrose lad on board

The Glasgow steel full-rigged ship Falklandbank was uninsurable in Lloyd's yesterday, underwriters refusing to accept any further lines on her. On Saturday the last rate paid to "cover" her was 94 guineas per cent, "total loss only"

The Falklandbank, which left Port Talbot on 9th November for Valparaiso, carried a cargo of South Wales coal and a crew of about 28 hands. The vessel was spoken in lat. 31 South, long.36 West in December, and that is the last news of her.

It is supposed that she foundered in the heavy gale off the River Plate at the end of December or has been destroyed by the spontaneous combustion of her coal cargo.

Including the cargo and all other interests the Falklandbank represents a value of nearly £25,000. She was of 1913 tons burden, built on the Clyde in 1894, classed 100 A1 at Lloyd's, and was owned by Messrs. Andrew Weir & Co, Hope Street, Glasgow.

The following is a list of some of the crew who were on board when the Falklandbank left Port Talbot:-

J.H.Robbins, captain
Thos. Laing, chief officer
Gerald Winton, second officer
Eric Prince, carpenter

....

Altogether there were 3 officers, 15 seamen, 5 apprentices, 5 others - total 28
Copied from worn press cutting Nov 13th 2014

....

Inspected 5 July 1906 Lloyd's register. Falklandbank No.37 in Missing Vessels book 1906-1913 . Sailing vessel. 1913 gross tonnage. Built 1894 Mackie and Thomson, Glasgow.

Posted missing 24 June 1908

Sailed Port Talbot for Valparaiso 9 Nov 1907

Arrived Montevideo 27 Dec 1907

Arthur Forsyth was one of the apprentices

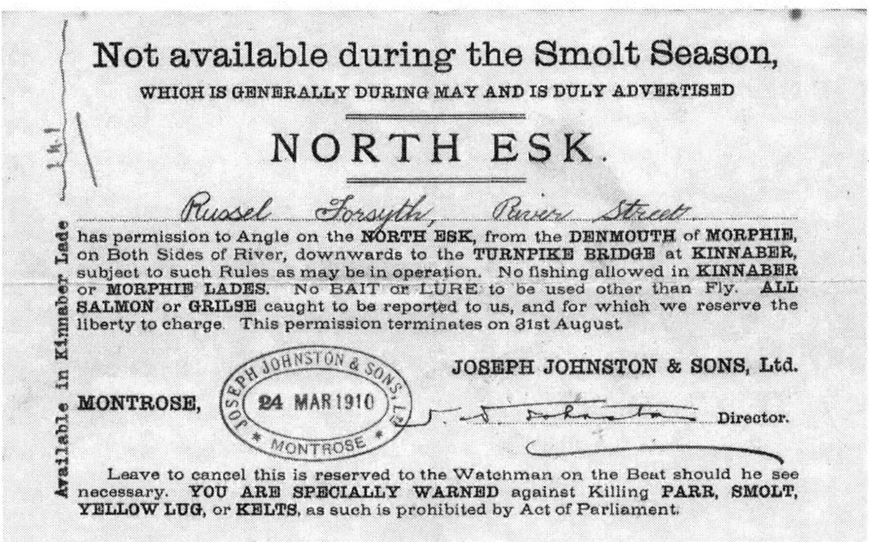

Not available during the Smolt Season,

WHICH IS GENERALLY DURING MAY AND IS DULY ADVERTISED

NORTH ESK.

Russel Forsyth, River Street

has permission to Angle on the **NORTH ESK**, from the **DENMOUTH** of **MORPHIE**, on Both Sides of River, downwards to the **TURNPIKE BRIDGE** at **KINNABER**, subject to such Rules as may be in operation. No fishing allowed in **KINNABER** or **MORPHIE LADES**. No BAIT or LURE to be used other than Fly. **ALL SALMON** or **GRILSE** caught to be reported to us, and for which we reserve the liberty to charge. This permission terminates on 31st August.

JOSEPH JOHNSTON & SONS, LTD. 24 MAR 1910 MONTROSE

JOSEPH JOHNSTON & SONS, Ltd.

MONTROSE, Director.

Leave to cancel this is reserved to the Watchman on the Beat should he see necessary. **YOU ARE SPECIALLY WARNED** against Killing **PARR, SMOLT, YELLOW LUG**, or **KELTS**, as such is prohibited by Act of Parliament.

Available in Kinnaber Lade

Rusty's fishing licence 1910

All the Forsyth boys had licences to fish in the North Esk. One was caught by the Bailiff for fishing without a licence.

The Spartan, John Forsyth's first ship

The Forsyths

Top left is John Forsyth, my grandfather. Top right is the eldest son Allan, my Uncle Allan, named Hadji after his time in Persia. On his right is his mother, Mary Heiton Forsyth, born Allan, my grandmother, called Mitherie by her children. Top left, next to his father is Arthur, the second son, lost at sea in 1907. On his right is Bessie, my Aunty Bee, a red head. In front are the two boys, Will on the right, Russell (Rusty, my father) on the left. The girl on my grandmother's right is unknown. The housekeeper or a mysterious relation?

4

1914 to 1919 – The First War

August 4th 1914 was the day the war began.

Greensmiths

There were immediate complications for George Greensmith. Two of his partners, Otto and Ernst, were born in Germany. Both had been naturalized well before the war and were British. But there was an upsurge of hatred for anything German and Schiff was a German name.

I joined Schroders the London merchant bank in 1970. One day at lunch Michael Verey, then head of Schroders, told us what happened when war broke out in 1914. All the biggest British merchant banks had substantial German and Russian business. Remittances from Germany and Russia stopped immediately. All the heads of the merchant banks were out of London at the beginning of August, mostly on their shooting estates in Scotland. It was clear on their return to London that they were all broke, with huge liabilities that could not be met. All the accepting houses were invited to meet at the Bank of England and discuss the situation. They met on August 5th. What do you do in a crisis? The answer was: form a committee. The Bank of England then agreed to provide the necessary funds to enable the accepting houses to meet their liabilities – on condition that the owners received no income themselves from their companies until the end of the war. This was the origin of the prestigious acceptance house committee that dominated the City until Margaret Thatcher's reforms many years later.

Schroders were a special case. Baron Bruno Schröder, the head of the firm, was a German. His well connected partner Henry Tiarks insisted with the Bank of England and the government that arrangements should be made for the immediate naturalization of Baron Bruno so that the business could continue to operate. He argued that it would be a disaster "if the doors of

Baron Schröder did not open on the following morning." Tiarks got his way. Schroders was already an important name in the City. On 7th August Baron Bruno was issued with a naturalisation certificate from the Home Secretary and a licence to reside and trade signed by King George V. (The umlaut was correct at the time but wisely dropped later).

There was another upsurge against all things German after the sinking of the Lusitania by a German submarine in May 1915. The Stock exchange instructed members of German birth not to attend until further notice and the London Chamber of Commerce required the resignation of German born members

This atmosphere of hate cannot have made things easy for Otto and Ernst and it is striking that both in due course received British awards, an MBE for Ernst and in Otto's case eventually, before the second war, a CBE.

We have no record of how Bourke Schiff fared during the first war, but it was a bad time.

When war broke out Reggie Greensmith was in Compiegne, in north France. This was uncomfortably close to the Franco-German border. He hastened back to the UK but his application to enlist was rejected, at 16 he was too young. Instead he joined, as a drummer boy, the unit his father George had joined; the National Guard City of London Volunteers.

The next year he tried again. He received a letter dated 20th August 1915 from the Director, Air Department, Admiralty. It refers to his appearance before the Selection Committee the previous day and states that, subject to his passing the medical test, he will be entered as soon as a vacancy occurs as a flight sub lieutenant on probation in the Royal Naval Air Service.

There were no tests of ability. It seems that it was good enough for the Admiralty that Reggie was well scrubbed and had been to a decent school.

The Admiralty wasted no time. Reggie was appointed Probationary Flight Sub-Lieutenant and directed to report on 5th September to the Commanding Officer, Whale Island, Portsmouth, for a short gunnery course in HMS Excellent. On completion of the course he was sent to Eastchurch in Kent to learn to fly. On the first day they were turned out of their beds early, to be on the airfield at first light. As they watched two trainee flights crashed and both pilots were killed.

Next in his father's scrap book is a letter dated 19th April 1916 from Lieutenant Caroll-Ward RNVR of the no.1 Royal Naval, Aeroplane Wing,

Dunkirk. It is addressed to Reggie's father and assures him his son, now in France, is popular in the mess and doing well.

Two weeks later, on 4th May, a telegram was delivered to the Greensmiths at 33 Inverness Terrace, Bayswater:

"Regret inform you Flight Sub-Lieutenant Greensmith missing after attack on enemy aerodrome this morning. Letter follows".

Reggie was missing, lost but, as it turned out, alive. The first confirmation of this was a telegram to his parents dated 17th May from 's-Gravenhage in the Netherlands:

"Can you please order four white flannel trousers and shirts dress suit patent white shoes light overcoat coloured shirts love Reggie Greensmith"

The telegram is legendary in family history.

So what happened to end Reggie's flying career? An extract from a Dutch newspaper seems as accurate as we can get:

"The aeroplane which landed at Cadzand in the so-called Old Swim was English. On the evening of the 3rd inst. The order was given to ascend at about 1 o'clock with about forty aeroplanes in order to bombard Zeebrugge and if possible the coastal batteries. As soon as they reached their object they were heavily bombarded which however did not prevent them dropping a number of bombs. The English aviator had dropped a number. Owing to the violent bombardment and the darkness, he lost his way and flew as far as Flushing, where he was shot at by the Dutch navy, after which he returned. He noticed however that his engine ran hot and was forced to make a descent. He saw in the early morning light a number of Dutch flags and decided to alight, but noticed when he had landed that he was still on Belgian territory. The German frontier guards shot at him, but he managed to escape across the Dutch frontier. He still tried to put his plane on fire but did not succeed. The Germans rushed on to make him a prisoner. He jumped in the water and waded on until he was taken prisoner by our frontier guards. In the aeroplane were still a few bombs which he could not manage to drop. The interned aviator hales from London."

Reggie's great good luck was that the tide was out and he was therefore able to get round the end of the electrified fence which encircled all the rest of neutral Holland.

Letter to Reggie, interned, from the Mess he left behind

May.16

'My dear old Babe,

First of all to business

From	Wine Fund	51.40
	Tobacco Fund	107.00
	Mess	12.70

		171.10

The change is for luck, do let me know if it is not all O.K.

We miss you round, with your 179 degree feet!! What rotten luck for you, but we are always hoping to see you turn up here with a thrilling story of how I escaped from Holland, by Louis de Rougemont. Your letter to the C.O. has not fetched up and at present we know nothing about you.

There have been *beaucoup de raids* lately, speaking both actively and passively and we have not had a whole night in for five nights what with bombing and being bombed. The garden is beginning to look capital: all the seeds are up tho' not fearfully strong yet and the gazon[1] is looking a treat. I will send a photo of it in a couple of months time or so.

I got home to England (?briefly) a week ago and spent two capital nights in London owing to bad weather. I danced each night up till 4.30 and caught the 5.50 down to Dover and failed to get any sleep for two nights and then flew the Channel. I found the loveliest little thing that God ever put skirts onto. 'nough said we have fixed up a trip on the broads for next leave: How do you find the Dutchesses?

We have had casualties in the neighbourhood as published in the papers. The gramophone has arrived and it is a great boon. It is simply lovely sitting on the verandah at night listening to it and imbibing cocktails made by Ciro's (?) bartender.

Well, no time for more. Everybody sends love and condolences and Brackley says the girl at the chateau (words crossed out) but there he will tell you all about that himself.

1 'gazon' – lawn

Goodbye so sorry for you best love from Mack

Brackley says this is most unfair.

—

Reggie was interned in Holland for the rest of the war. Surprisingly however he was allowed to visit England on parole to visit his aged mother. Furthermore he was able to arrange for a fellow internee, an Australian or New Zealander, who had no aged mother to hand, to accompany him to England on parole. My grandfather had asked a waitress from his local ABC restaurant in the City to act as his girlfriend and the excuse for the parole. The airman took her to dinner before his brief time in London ended.

During their time as internees a (mainly British?) group of officers used to meet at a bar in the Hague. When the owner decided to change location he asked the officers to suggest a new name. The bar was relocating to a site behind the Parliament building in The Hague. The officers suggested "The House of Lords". The name remained until the Second War.

For part of his internment he was employed by Royal Dutch Shell and learnt Dutch.

He said he had the time of his life in Holland – dancing, tennis, sailing, motoring. He said he longed to go to France and fly again. His father said better a lieutenant alive than an admiral dead.

Internment ended Reggie's war

Forsyths

The first of the Forsyth family to enlist in the Army was Allan, my father's eldest brother. As already explained, as soon as war was declared he cycled from Montrose to Dundee to volunteer. However, following his time in Ceylon, he was declared malaria ridden and told to go away and get fit. The next year he was accepted. He joined the Royal Artillery and went to France, where he was wounded.

Later he was sent to Persia to join the South Persian Rifles, known as SPRI, a unit effectively part of the British Army in India. This regiment was formed after Percy Sykes mission to Mesopotamia in March 1916.

This mission followed two disasters – the final withdrawal from Gallipoli in January 1916 and the surrender of the British force at Kut-al-Amara in April 1916.

Percy Sykes after the war was famous, or notorious, for negotiating the Sykes-Picot pact, determining French and British spheres of interest in the Middle East. He raised the South Persian Rifles, at its peak 8000 men, and led it until after the end of the war. It was formed to maintain order in Southern Persia, to counter German activities there and prevent Germany establishing a presence on the sensitive borders of India and beyond. German strategy, in the early stages of the war, was to seek, with its Ottoman allies, to raise the Moslem world in a holy war against the British in India; and to disrupt the supply of Persian oil to the Royal Navy. The German agent Wasserman, the German Lawrence, had some success. Other German agents reached Afghanistan, but their efforts were frustrated.

After the Russian revolution in 1917 the Russians, and hostile Persian tribes, replaced the Germans as the major threat to stability in the area, and to British interests. The Anglo-Iranian Oil company, which became BP, was formed in 1919, with the Admiralty supporting the British Government's investment.

Northern Persia was a Russian sphere of interest, just as the South was British. After the revolution Soviet agents began infiltrating the British zone and it was because of this that the SPRI was not immediately dissolved.

Sykes, later Sir Percy, was proud of his regiment. He claimed it marched over 5000 miles in the course of the war, more than any other.

In the only picture I ever saw of him in uniform, Uncle Allan, young, suntanned and handsome in cavalry breeches, held a handsome horse. The picture was always at his wife's bedside

In 1919 the British were involved in the third Afghan war. The Indian army, of which SPRI was a part, was short of officers. As a result Allan as an artillery officer was directed to Afghanistan to take charge of Indian mountain artillery. SPRI was disbanded eventually in 1923.

Allan, as Captain, was awarded the MBE, for what his brother Russell called "his dirty work in Persia". Allan had distinguished himself by establishing good relations with a local tribal chief and persuading him gently, over a dinner or two, to keep to his alliance with the British.

However this is what his son Ian told me:

"From what I remember Dad telling me he went directly from the Western Front to the North West Frontier. He was in command of a troop of mountain artillery. There was an attack through one of the passes towards Kandahar. The terrain was very difficult. When he wanted to go in a certain direction he consulted his Head Muleteer: the Head Muleteer consulted the Head Mule. If the Head Mule decided to go down the trail, the rest followed!

While with the South Persia Rifles he was instructed to go and placate an important Mullah whose vineyard had been vandalized by levies linked to the SPR. So Dad swotted up his phrasebook and set off on horseback. As he approached the Mullah's area he noticed the quality of the sheep were much better than in other areas. So, having met the Mullah and "wept at the sight of your desecrated vineyard" he was invited to a meal, where he commented on the fine quality of the lamb that was served, and the quality of the stock he had seen on the way in.

Dad's CO was so impressed that the Mullah had been placated, and was now co-operating with the British, that he recommended Dad for the MBE"

Will was the next of the three Montrose brothers. He also joined the Artillery but in 1918 was transferred to the newly formed RAF as an artillery spotter. His plane was shot down in July 1918, he was killed. He is buried in Motor Car Corner cemetery in Ploegstraat in Belgium, close to the border with France. It is so called because it was the point at which motor vehicles turned back before the front line.

I was told that my father, Russell, stationed nearby went to visit his brother's airfield. The squadron's planes were off on a mission. Only one did not return.

This was the second great blow for John and Mary.

Russell and Will were great friends. Russell was 16 at the beginning of the war. I have a copy of his letter of 17th April 1915 addressed to the Officer Commanding, Officers Training Corps at St Andrews. He says:

"I beg to make application to enter the unit commanded by you. I am an apprentice with Messrs Mackay Irons & Co C.A. Dundee and am eighteen years of age. In normal times I would matriculate at the University College Dundee in the course of a year for classes in Scots Law, but am anxious to enter the OTC now in order to get on service as soon as I am sufficiently trained. I am keen to follow in my brother's footsteps who was gazetted last May (?) out of the Edinburgh OTC.

Trusting you will give my application due consideration, I am sir yours faithfully, H Russell Forsyth"

One evening when Murray and I were staying at Hardmead, Uncle Allan's Bridge of Earn home, I was reading Herodotus as part of my University studies. I came across an account of sheep in Persia with fat flabby tails. Herodotus reported that to protect the tails the shepherds made trolleys on which the tails could ride. I said to Uncle Allan what nonsense we had to read. He said it was not nonsense, he had seen the sheep with their fat tails made safe on trolleys.

Allan Forsyth,Uncle Allan, Rusty's eldest brother,
Captain in the South Persian Rifles, probably 1918

Uncle Allan ready for Polo

William Forsyth, Uncle Will,
artillery spotter RAF, killed July 1918

Henry Russell Forsyth, my father, Rusty,
Lieutenant Royal Field Artillery

Rusty probably joined the Royal Field Artillery later in 1915. Certainly he was at the front in October 1916. He wrote a letter then to his young cousin Hamish, referring to "we mortar men". He gives advice on how to react to German shellfire. If it's a "sausage", travelling end on, and is aimed directly at you, don't stop to think, run. If it is not aimed directly at you don't worry. You can be an interested spectator. He explains that "rum jars", which turn over all the time, are different and have a shorter range.

This letter is the only surviving record of those times.

Russell was hit by a machine gun bullet in the foot and sent back to blighty, to the officers hospital at Eaton Hall. He returned to France but was in Montrose at the end of the war. He said he was sorry he could not be with his men. During his time in France he had an arrangement with the saddler in the High Street Montrose for the regular supply of rugby balls for his mortar men.

For a time he was stationed at Leiston in Suffolk, where he was again wounded – falling off his bicycle!

At the end of the war he was sent to Cologne as part of the army of occupation. He went on leave to Lille in France, staying at a villa in the Rue de l'hippodrome in Lambersat, on the outskirts of the town. The house survived the first war but was destroyed in the second. The owner was Madame Haines, a widow, who lived there with her daughter. Her husband was the architect of the Theatre Sebastopol in Lille (still surviving, under another name). Russell was clearly fond of the two of them. I have the postcards they exchanged, stamped with the mark of the censor and sent to Russell in his anti-aircraft unit in Cologne. Russell subsequently sent them a box of chocolates every year at Christmastime. They would not have known why the chocolates stopped coming in 1941. I have never been able, for example through the Municipal authorities in Lille, to track down the Haines family or its descendants. Someone even now must have a distant memory of the young Scots officer who came to stay at the end of the First War and sent a box of chocolates every year afterwards.

Grandfather John Forsyth died in November1916. Grandfather George Greensmith was too old to join the Regular Army, but, as mentioned already, he joined the National Guard City of London Volunteers., where he was briefly joined by his son Reggie. They filled sandbags for anti-aircraft defence in Hyde Park. Later he was a Special Policeman, on guard at Buckingham Palace. He successfully prevented a drunken American from penetrating the Palace defences. We still have, somewhere, his elegant truncheon.

Finally in November 1918 the war ended and the lights went on again in Europe

Rusty's letter to his young nephew Hamish

Wednesday 18th October 1916, British Expeditionary Force, from the front.

My Dear Hamish,

You must think I am an old frost for not writing to you sooner and after all my only excuses are stress of work and laziness.

This is not to be a letter in any sense of the word but only a note to let you know that I haven't forgotten about you altogether. I was in awe of your canoe construction. But look here, Hamish, you are not to let Francis correct (?) or in any way revise your letters for at least if you keep it up or you'll beat her to sticks at writing

By the way I have a letter for Francis in my pocket. I always keep a letter until I write some sort of a reply and then immediately consume it in the flames. Sound scheme is it not?

Well I must get on with some little news because I don't have much time. You see we are on the move again which means little time for letter writing. I thought we had settled nicely for the winter and even had a distant chance of leave but all that is buckled up with this move. I guess it is now at long last our turn to let the Hun know that we have some stuffing in us. We have waited long but I think our chance is coming this time. I am only afraid we mortar people wont have much to do as our ammunition is rather cumbersome.

You would laugh I think if you saw our crude little gun. Though the calibre is only 2" we throw a 5lb. The explanation is that the bomb itself is round and has a 20 … tail of 2" diameter so you can guess that it is the tail of the bomb that goes on to the bore. We fairly knock the old Hun's trenches about. It is fine to see boards, bricks and earth flying about – oh most satisfactory! We burst all his wire entanglements to bits in fact when we set out we can keep him fairly on the hop! Then when he gets annoyed he begins to retaliate with "minnies". You hear a "ponk" and immediately look up for the "sausage" or "rum jar" coming lobbing over. The "sausage" has a long range, goes fairly high and travels end on all the time: while the rum jar (so called because of its shape) has a shorter range and turns over and over in the air. Well you can see them coming as I said before and if he is making for you don't stop to think but run as hard as you can to one flank or the other. If Minnie is not coming straight for you, no need to worry you are only an interested spectator. Now, there are some tips if you ever come out here, which I hope will never come to pass. We knocked out a "Minnie", seven direct hits with a 50 pounder and he didn't speak again – neither would you if you got seven of our own matter on top!

Now Hamish I don't have time to wander on to(x- y -1) pages but if you take the number of pages I have written and multiply by eleven teen, take the whole to the 70th power and thence to multiply by minus 1 you will arrive perhaps at the exact number of pages I should in more peaceful times have written to you. Got that, sunny Jim? How is your German getting on? You are a regular don at that, aren't you, or is it French? If you are to be an engineer, in fact anything, you'll have to swat maths and all the rest – Take it from one that didn't. Now old man I must hop. You'll be the big man at home now that bruvver Bill has started out on his career. I still owe Francis a letter – the photographs she sent me were topping.

Hope you are all fit and "in the pink" and not working too hard. Meantime cheerio with love from your silly old cousin

RUSS

Reginald Eustace Greensmith RNAS

Probationary Flight Lieutenant, Royal Naval Air Squadron. My Uncle Reggie, 18 years old, with his father, my grandfather, George Greensmith. Inverness Terrace, London, 1915.

One of his squadron's planes. An airfield near Dunkirk 1916?

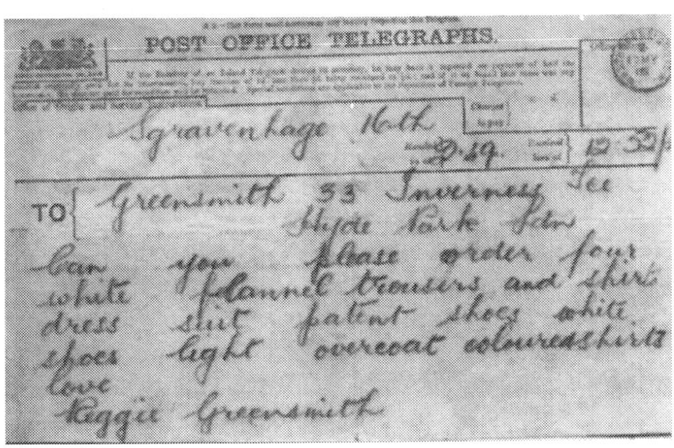

POST OFFICE TELEGRAPHS.

Sgravenhage 16th
2.49 12.32

TO Greensmith 53 Inverness Tce
Hyde Park Ldn

Can you please order four
white flannel trousers and shirts
dress suit patent shoes white
shoes light overcoat colouredshirts
love
Reggie Greensmith

His telegram to his parents from 's-Gravenhage, 17 May 1916.

5

John and Mary Forsyth and family

Grandfather John's business was coal – coal and the carriage of coal. Coal after all was the fuel of the day - fuel for homes, fuel for the railways and fuel for the steamships that came to the port of Montrose. John was a modestly successful businessman and a respected citizen.

At some stage he went into partnership with a sea captain friend and bought a vessel, and perhaps more than one. My cousin, Wee Allan (Uncle Allan's son), remembers a picture of a ship, "The Spartan", pointed out as one of his grandfather's.

John became a pillar of the church. Following the great schism of 1843 (The Disruption), when the Church of Scotland split, and all the dissenting ministers were dispossessed, John was one of those who made it his life's work to raise, for the Free Church of Scotland, the necessary funds for the building of new churches and paying the ministers' wages. Throughout the 19th century and beyond there were constant realignments of the Presbyterian churches of Scotland and finally in 1904 there was a House of Lords decision awarding to the residual Free Church of Scotland all the lands and properties of the original Free Church, the Calvinistic rump henceforth being known as the "Wee Frees". John and his fellows were thunderstruck by the House of Lords decision. They walked the Links (the Montrose seaside golf course) for a long time, deliberating what they should do. They resolved they would start again and rebuild the church they had spent most of their lifetime struggling to create.

John was a stern father. He firmly believed in the benefits of sea bathing and it was his strict rule that the boys should bathe regularly from spring time to autumn. On one occasion my father and his brother Will went bathing and saw a bather out at sea in difficulties. Between them they managed to place the swimmer on a raft and Will, as the strongest swimmer, swam to get help. Eventually they got the stricken party to shore. They then raced for home (at Panmure Cottage, over the road from the end of the Links) knowing how serious a crime it was, in their father's eyes, to be late for mealtimes. At Church the next Sunday one of the congregation approached John to thank him for the action of his sons who had saved his life. John was amazed. The boys had not dared to try to explain the reason for their lateness – even if it was to save a life.

At meals the family were served in order, round the table. My father being the youngest was often afraid there would be nothing left. Complaint was not possible.

—

John died aged 61 in November 1916. Mary was born in 1861 and was 26 when they married. She died aged 83 in1944.

Their deaths are recorded on a memorial plaque in the South East corner of the furthest section of the New (non religious) Cemetery in Montrose. The names of their sons have been added.

—

Mary (my grandmother, Mitherie to her children) lived on long after John. I remember her well, a tall grey haired lady, with a bun. She was very kind to me. She knew that mashed bananas, sugar and cream was a favourite, and when I went to tea at Pancot there was always a plate for me, often to my dismay hidden away at first, at least once on top of the wardrobe.

John left everything to his wife and when she died the property was distributed among her children. There was some dispute in law as to whether my mother or her children could inherit my father's share. This was resolved. Each of John's grandchildren received a little package of shares, about £1000. They had been invested over many years by prudent Scotttish solicitors in safe securities, municipal tramways for example, left far behind in the post war stock market boom. The legacies nevertheless were timely and appreciated.

The next Forsyth generation.

My Uncle Allan, the eldest of John and Mary's children, was born in 1888. He went to Agricultural College in Aberdeen. He was not a very strong child and for the sake of his health (suspected TB?) went to work with a farmer, somewhere to the north of Montrose. At 78 in 1966 he outlasted all the rest.

When I went to live in Islington, in 1961 or thereabouts, Uncle Allan said he knew Islington, in particular the Agricultural Hall. He had been there for the Caledonian Market Agricultural Show, when his Scottish employer was showing off his beasts. He would travel down by train with them from Scotland. He said in those days, before the First War, you were not permitted to drive cattle through the streets of Islington – mind you, he said, I don't suppose you are now. The beasts would be carted from the station to the Agricultural Hall and the herdsmen would bed down with them. Next morning they would be up early, brushing them down and preparing them for the show. At noon he said a great cry went up "the pubs are open!" This was shocking to the Scots herdsmen. They had never known pubs open on a Sunday.

Uncle Allan heard that we had a small vegetable bed in our Islington back garden. He sent me down some of his precious seed potatoes, "Auchmithie Ministers". Aunty Nan, his wife, said this was a great honour. I am afraid the prize Perthshire potatoes did not prosper in our sooty little patch. Despite enquiries, then and afterward, I was never able to replace them. I made a special visit to Auchmithie, an isolated seaside village not far to the South of Montrose. I asked about the tatties at the inn. The mother of the landlady had a faint recollection; but opinion in the bar was that neither the minister nor his tatties had survived.

Some time before the First War Uncle Allan went out (I believe on some Government scheme) to be a tea planter, in what was then Ceylon, part of the British Empire.

He must have returned to Montrose sometime before the war since, if I am right, it was he, and not one of his brothers, who cycled to Dundee to enlist on 4th August 1914, the day war was declared.

The Burgess Family

Dr. James Burgess (seated, centre) with his wife (seated centre-right); 3 sons, standing from left: Arthur, Cecil, and Charles; and 3 daughters, seated from left: Nettie, Edith, and cousin May, who married Professor Nielson of Smith College, Massachusetts (seated on right)

We used to have tea with cousin Nettie in her Edinbugh flat. Scrabble followed tea. James Burgess was my father's uncle. He was Director of Archaeology in India. Cecil was Professor of Architecture at Edmonton, Alberta.

6

The Twenties

The war ended on November 11th 1918.

It ended with the collapse of Germany. The Kaiser escaped to neutral Holland and never returned.

Reggie returned to London after his internment in Holland. He received from the RNAS his negligible back pay, but at least he was alive. His only experience apart from his time with the RNAS was his employment in Holland with Shell

Western educated Sun Yat Sen was President of China. He had come to power after the overthrow of the last Manchu Emperor in 1911. He became first President of the new Republic of China on 1st Jan 1912. He remained President until his death in March 1925.

China had taken no part in the 1914-1918 war, although it declared war on Germany in 1917, following the United States. It was under new management, and modernizing rapidly. To a young man looking for a job – Reggie was 21 in 1918 – China must have seemed a land of opportunity. Apart from financial prospects, Shanghai was a notoriously exciting place to live.

Reggie stayed a brief period in London with his parents, and then went East to Shanghai, most likely in 1920. Perhaps with the help of his father, he became a stock-jobber on the Shanghai Stock Exchange

In November 1922 he married Lucy Craven, the daughter of a tea trader. Sometimes tea traders were rich – and Lucy's father would charter a railway coach to take the family on tour across the United States. Sometimes after a bad year they were penniless. But they mostly survived to live long lives.

The engagement was not without its complications. Sometime before they were formally engaged Lucy had apparently let it be known that they were. Reggie nevertheless did the decent thing and uncomplainingly went through with it. He received his compensation many years later when after he divorced

Lucy to marry his mistress who then married Reggie's best friend. Reggie and Lucy then remarried.

Elaine, meanwhile, had left St Cuthbert's. The boarders earlier, in 1919, had moved to Southbourne with Miss Fuller, as headmistress. In March 1921 Elaine was 17 and in the following year she was made head girl. Miss Fuller thought she should go on to Oxford and took Elaine there. They stayed at the Mitre in the High Street and called on the Principal of Lady Margaret Hall. But Elaine's parents thought learning languages would be more practical.

Elaine went to France to learn French, at first to a language school at Le Vesinet, close to Paris. But she said there were too many young English girls, and she was not learning enough. It was arranged she should leave Le Vesinet and move to Tours. This was a happy time, cycling down the Loire valley, visiting the chateaux, learning German as well as French.

While at Vesinet she went to Paris in November 1922 to see Sarah Bernhardt in La Gloire. Make-up concealed her age – Sarah was 74. She died weeks later in March 1923. Black horses led the open coffin through crowded streets to the Père Lachaise cemetery.

Elaine's real love however was German and during the twenties she spent much time in Germany, walking in the Black Forest, staying in youth hostels, making many friends. I have her youth hostel card –"Reichverband fur Jugendheberge". These were exciting times for young Germans, and the new youth hostel movement was a sign of the times. German youth were moving away from the shadow of the war and there was hope for a new future. After a day's walk there was singing in the evening and Elaine claimed to know the songs better than most of the rest.

She corresponded for many years with girlfriends of those days. Most of the letters from Germany were in German, to "Meine liebe Elaine"

The two most constant letter writers were Elsa Rau and Liesel Schmelz – see German letters attached.

Elsa's first surviving letter is dated 28 December 1925, and is from Munich. The last is dated 11 May 1939. This last is written in English from Utrecht in Holland. Elaine had written to her from Hong Kong saying she was returning in 1939 via Berlin and hoping to meet her there. The letter arrived too late, but when Elsa eventually received it she wrote to Elaine saying she expected soon to be in England and hoped to meet her there. "It will be thrilling to see you again as mother of such a big family. I am sure you are still the bright and laughing, jolly Elaine that I knew and loved in Munich."

"Meantimes my home has not only been broken up but I have also lost my country and this is hard in spite of everything I had to go through there."

She hopes to find a job in England but for the time being is staying in her sister's house in Holland.

The first of the many letters, from Liesel and Elsa is dated July 22 1927, but there may have been some earlier. All are from Saarbrucken, Metzerstrasse 45. The second last is dated April 22 1936. It ends with "Herzliche Grusse, Ihre Liesel Schmelz", followed by a handwritten note "Mein Mann ist auch ein brauner Soldat Adolf Hitlers. Ein S.A,Mann" The next letter, dated July 10th 1937, with photographs of her children, ends "Viele liebe Grusse und ein kraftiges Heil Hitler, ihre treue Liesel Schmelz"(many loving greetings and a hearty Heil Hitler from your true friend Liesel)

It seems most likely that Elsa was Jewish and suffered for it, at the hands of Liesel's people. It also explains Elaine's ambivalent attitude to Germany during the war and her doubts about German atrocities. These were not the warm-hearted Germans she knew.

She had spent some time much earlier, in June and July 1924, as an escort with St Barnabas Pilgrimage, taking groups of mothers from England to visit War Graves in France and Belgium. Elaine was timid in public places so she was always very proud that on one of these trips she had spoken out. Some German mothers boarded the coach where the English mothers had taken their places. The latter protested vehemently at the presence of the German mothers. Elaine said the English mothers should be ashamed of themselves. They had all suffered the sadness of loss.

Reggie and Lucy were by now, in 1925, settled in Shanghai. Wallis Simpson had arrived in 1924 and lived scandalously apart from her American Navy husband

Ann, their first child, was born on 10th March 1925. Jane her sister, at first known as Bunty, arrived two years later, on 31 March 1927.

Sun Yat Sen, the founder and first president of the Republic of China, made a significant speech on Pan-Asianism in Kobe in 1924. He died in 1925.

He was succeeded by Chiang Kai Shek. He had at first accepted Communists in his party, the Kuo Min Tang (Chinese nationalist party). But in 1927 he expelled the Communists in a brutal coup, the beginnings of a civil war. In 1928 he formed a new national government in Nanking.

These were, evidently, turbulent times in China. Probably because of this Reggie and Lucy moved from Shanghai to Hong Kong in 1927.

Elaine came to visit them in 1928. She had already travelled extensively.

In January 1927 George, writing to his son Reggie, says that the firm had had "the best year ever". They were expecting profits "between £80,000 to £90,000". However he had spent a good deal – rewarding the staff and paying for Elaine's world trip. In November, nearing the end of this trip, she had cabled home from San Francisco - and a few days, later in January, she was off to Munich for "3 or 4 months".

It must have been on this 1926 world trip that she first visited Japan. With a girlfriend she went walking in the mountains. The girlfriend had a wooden leg which broke. As a result they had to stay in a mountain village while the village carpenter made a new leg. The girlfriend had a spare wooden leg, but it was out of reach, with her husband, an Australian submarine commander, somewhere under the South Pacific.

Elaine had a fine singing voice, and had sung at London's Wigmore Hall. On this occasion in Japan she went to a geisha party and was asked to sing to the geishas.

It was also on this trip that she met Clifford Pope. They travelled by train from San Francisco. On 29 November 1926 he wrote a delightful all-American note to her, from Savannah, Georgia. A copy of this letter is attached.

The General Strike

George's letter of 11th May 1926

My dear Reggie and Lucy,

We are right in the midst of one of the greatest social upheavals of modern times.

By the time you receive this there is no doubt at all it will be all over. I hope you have not been unduly scared about the welfare of all of us. This last week has been very reminiscent of the early days of the War. All soldiers and guards at the Palace in war kit – and a great rush by everyone to enlist for some service or the other. All the parks taken over by the military or civil commissioners ...and transport of necessaries being carried on almost entirely by motor lorries. Last Saturday mother and I were returning home from a West End stroll and just as we got to Sloane Square there was a convoy of armoured cars and lorries -140 of the latter – the whole length of Sloane street, just proceeding on their way to the docks. Each lorry had 5 men in khaki, rifles and steel helmetsa rather impressive sight. There was a rush the first few days by lots of people to get in foodstuff candles, matches etc but this has now abated. There have been a few collisions between hooligans and keepers of peace and order but I hazard a guess there will be fewer mortalities than would occur in a fracas between French students. The really astonishing thing has been the cheerfulness and good feeling between all classes – hospital work, Special constabulary. All the cars one sees seem to have and the buses have just started running again the last 2/e days by voluntary drivers, with a policeman seated at his side and ...says he is arrived .. by the chalked inscriptions on them all

Palace Hotel

Lucerne, 8 July 1926

My Darling Elaine,

We have just received yours of the 26th May, giving descriptions of the last part of your trip to Japan and some of your escapades at Hong Kong. I think you must go a bit mad at times, but I hope you keep your head and don't do anything too foolish.

We are still having nice time here, altho the weather has been pretty bad these last 2 days. Yesterday was a "soaker". Anyway we managed in the morning to get as far as the Kursaal where they have a very good Hungarian Orchestra. They have a wonderful "Cymbalist" (an instrument like a dulcimer) and after the concert we, and 2 Americans, went up – after the people had left – and persuaded him to play us one or two pieces. His effect and execution was wonderful.

At 5 o'clock it ceased raining for while so we got out for a walk. The Cathedral has a very fine organ – the finest in fact I have ever heard, and each evening there is a recital from 6 to 7. So at 6 o'clock we dropped in again. Connected with the big organ there is an echo organ- The large one can be very powerful and the effects produced are really wonderful. Bugle calls and echo, thunder, lightning and pattering rain – the latter not a musical note, but some kind of a gadget which first made us think the rain outside had again started heavier than ever, until the repetition disillusioned us.

This morning the weather was not quite so bad, so we went and did a little shopping. Last night I had a rather cheery wire from the office, on the strength of which I bought mother a piece of lacework on which she had set longing eyes for the last few days. All the lacework is very beautiful here and I cant drag mother away from the shops. I treated myself to 8 very nice linen – coloured borders – handkerchiefs - - and also a few for Cambridge and Jeannie Porter

This afternoon we went to Vitznau – oh! By the way I also bought M a little black ribbon with marquesite attachment to be worn round the neck in the evening

We had a nice trip on the lake to Vitznau –the steamers are so beautifully clean and comfortable – you'll remember those on L. Geneva. We had tea there and wandered around for an hour or so – bought another lace motif (I think that's the name) and returned about 6pm.

Quite the best trip we have had so far was on Monday last to Engelberg. It was a beautiful day. We started about 10 am. Steamer to Stans?, thence by rail through beautiful valleys – with waterfalls etc etc climbing gradually higher to E. After lunch there we took a funicular to ? and caught a very fine view to Titlis – in shape something like Castor and Pollux – you'll remember them.

There has been an International Cours Hippique held here lasting 3 or 4 days. We went on Sunday afternoon last. All the elite were there including King of the Belgians. Competitors were chiefly Belgian, Italian, German. Swiss. The jumping was very good and sometimes quite exciting.

Mother is not doing so well with the language. Translation is not so difficult. She can translate words like "Motorboote" "Konzert" "Elektric" "Musik" etc but she has now given up trying pronunciation. On the steamer yesterday she would refer to two places we called at on the way "Gersau" and "Weggis" as Gizzard and Haggis.

I brought my golf clubs along with me but have only played one round – with the Pro. The course is beautifully situated right up on the mountain side but as a golf course not too good. However I did not play too badly. As a matter of fact my golf has improved quite a lot the last 2 months. I have an important match to play when I get back. You'll remember Stanley Viall whom we met at Newquay. A friend of his offered to bet 50 pounds he would beat any other member (Bramshot) of 24 h'ca. So I was selected and about a dozen or so of members have taken part of the bet – either have taken part of the bet – either 1 2 or 5 pounds – and the match is to come off some time in August.

We have just received a letter from Mrs Huntingdon from Lake Geneva. She saw a Mr and Mrs G had arrived at the Palace Lucerne and wondered whether it could be us. Vivienne is anxious to know what you are doing. Mother will be dropping her a line later.

You seemed a little distressed in your last letter that business was so bad here. As a matter of fact we haven't had a bad ½ year. Not so good as the previous one but not so bad considering all the labour troubles we have had.

Oh I must tell you another little faux pas of Mother's ! The other evening the waiter said "Would madam have a liqueur" She said she would like a "ceinture". The waiter looked dismayed. We discovered she meant a Cointreau.

Mrs Howard's father died a few weeks ago in Paris.

Mother I think told you Ernst Schiff lost their daughter suddenly – about two months old.

To fill up this page. Here's a little problem.A Scotsman wanted a drink which cost 9d. He only had 6d in his pocket. He pawned this for 5d, sold the ticket for 4d and got his drink.

Not a word in any of your letters as to when you are returning.

Thank Lucy very much for her letter which we received here 2 days ago. We have quite forgotten Reggie's hand writing. But this will come along again, I know, as soon as he has something cheerful to talk about.

Much love from us both to you all – a kiss for little Ann. The photos are excellent

Your affec Dad

Across the USA with Clifford Pope.

Letter from Clifford Pope, Savannah, Georgia, to Miss Greensmith 29 Nov 1926

Dear Miss Greensmith,

Now if I were writing to an American girl I would drop the "miss" but I am sure you would consider me "fresh" so I wont dare. At any rate such matters are of little importance either way you take them.

I found my sister waiting for me in New York when I arrived early Thanksgiving morning. We went out into the country and had a fine day. She went in swimming but I didn't have the courage! There was ice on the water. Would you have dared?

Because of family complications of an uninteresting nature I came on South the day after thanksgiving and will have to remain in Georgia until January.

From Chicago to New York I had a very lonesome trip all by myself and became quite depressed until a vaudeville show in Buffalo cheered me up. I had to wait there four hours so really I might have gone on with you to Buffalo and Niagara. However I should not feel so sure about the "might" as I figured up afterwards that I had dogged your footsteps for six consecutive days and you surely must have needed needed a change – putting it mildly. Perhaps you are wondering if all Americans of "21" are quite as persistent! I assure you they are not. You may have the satisfaction of knowing that I consider my recent trip across the continent by far the most enjoyable one I've ever had – as well as the most instructive. You taught me to "See America First"!

I am wondering how you are getting along at 965! Of course you are too busy to stop to write? If not a letter would be highly appreciated as I am really interested to know how things went with you from Chicago on. If you have forgiven me for being so "unfair" about squandering wads of money upon you I shall be gratified to know it. Just think, the US$2.00 or less squandered in Chicago might have been added to my old age pension. What waste!!

I do hope that New York will not bore you as much as it did Mr Moon but then if you can get a "kick" out of small western towns

New York should give you a real jolt. Please excuse all this cheap American wit.

By the way I heard that one town on or near the Santa Fe railroad out West is exactly like they used to be - wild and lawless – and that one man actually started a store in a piano box! Recall the picture that we saw in Chicago before I disgraced you by forcing you into the hashhouse.

On my way to the train. While walking down Michigan Ave., I passed a Page and Shaw shop and thought "why didn't you spend a few minutes there just now instead of in the station"

The Grand Canyon pictures have not come but I will send them along later.

I hope you will meet one or two modern American flappers as they are most amusing and entertaining if you take them in the proper spirit. I was strolling with one down town today. She met a man and said "Hello Boots", this in Clifford – by the way "Boots, what is your last name!"

That's the American style, why bother to remember the name that no one uses any more. America is truly the "land of the free" I know this sounds common to your English mind but then you are not very English in most ways.

There is a holy, pink-eyed albino, Indian baby elephant in the Bronx zoo which you should not miss. Mr Tooney could tell you all about him –it? – and I am sure he is much like the conductor and other train men (one porter excepted!) That porter was fresh.

I must close now after thanking you very much for escorting me all the way from Frisco and then to the most dangerous and wild city in America, and for giving me the opportunity of becoming acquainted with the first English girl on my list of feminine acquaintances.

Please drop me at least a few lines sometime

Very sincerely,

Clifford Pope

PS Mr and Mrs HORACE Andrew Davis ANNOUNCE THE MARRIAGE OF THEIR DAUGHTER Sarah Haydock to Clifford Hillhouse Pope on 8th September 1928 at New Canaan, Connecticut

He ends by thanking her very much for escorting him safely "from Frisco and (Dodge City), then the most dangerous and wild city in America", and for giving him thc opportunity of becoming acquainted with the first English girl on my list of feminine acquaintances" It was not the most elegant end but the exchange continued with the last letter, dated 29 October 1927, prompted by a post card from her, addressed simply to "Dear Elaine". After December his address would be "c/o Am Mus Nat. Hist NYC"

Years later my wife, Jacki, took me to see an exhibition on Mongolia in North London. Mongolia was Jacki's territory not mine but over the entrance to the exhibition was a stretched–out photograph of a long line of dust covered cars setting off across the Gobi desert. I was told this was the famous American trans Gobi mission in the 1920's looking for dinosaur eggs. I said that I knew all about it, my mother had a boyfriend who was on the mission – and was probably in one of the long line of cars in the picture. Jacki was much distressed at this intrusion of mine into her own yurt infested territory.

I never knew anything more of the American boy friend, but reading through the package of letters my mother preserved, one, dated 15 December 1926, has a scribbled note at the head of it "C/o after december Am. Mus. Nat .Hist. .Y.C.

In 1928 or 1929 she set off again to the East, principally to visit Reggie and Lucy, and her young nieces, in Hong Kong

She came by way of Singapore, to see her boy friend Cecil, assistant editor of the Malayan Mail in Kuala Lumpur. He wrote many passionate letters to her and passionately wanted to marry her. He continued to write to her - "I adore you" always - until mid 1929.

There was another passionate boy friend, Clive Gallup. This was a relationship which always haunted my mother. They had met in France. He was an undergraduate, I believe, at Oxford. He played the piano, he read a lot, they had much to discuss. He asked Elaine to marry him. But he fell ill. Elaine said they should leave aside thoughts of marriage until he was better. He wrote many letters to her. He did not get better. He was part paralysed and needed full time nursing care. In 1928 he died. His mother wrote to Elaine, knowing how fond of her Clive had been, thanking her for her kindness.

On this occasion Elaine travelled on from Singapore to stay with Reggie and Lucy in Hong Kong. It was there she met Russell.

On a tram journey in Hong Kong Elaine was much impressed when the conductor refused to accept payment from Russell for his ticket because of his previous great kindness to the conductor.

The original intention was that Elaine should return by way of Singapore, but her father did not entirely approve of Cecil and sent Elaine a return ticket from Hong Kong to the United States, then overland to New York, then back across the Atlantic to England. Elaine did not return via Singapore.

In New York she stayed with the Schiffs in one of the last private houses on 5th Avenue. The Schiffs gave her a book on Benjamin Franklin which we still have.

Disaster in 1930.

At some time in 1930 Elaine took her mother on a motoring trip through the South of England. In the course of it they received a telegram from George. "Catastrophe! Returrn at once"

Elaine and Lizzie returned at once to the apartment at 155 Sloane Street. My grandfather was slumped at his desk, in despair. "What is the matter? Lizzie asked. We are ruined, said George. Oh, said Lizzie, I thought you were ill!"

These are the words we remember her for, a legend in the family.

George was a stockbroker's clerk in 1896, when they were married. They had no assets then. Certainly George inherited nothing from his coachman father. But by 1906, when both were 30, they had moved from Balham to a new house at Weybourne. By 1907 George was sufficiently well known in stockbroking circles to be taken on as a partner in the newly formed stockbroking firm of Bourke Schiff. In 1909 he bought his second car, a smart new Renault landaulette for £650. With his initials (extra one guinea) engraved on the driver's door. There followed the lean years of the first world war and the boom years that followed in the twenties. It was then they bought their furniture from Maples (dark brown mahogany), their crockery from Goods and their full set of silver cutlery, probably from Harrods(Lizzie knew Mr Harrod).

And then came the crash. It was not a stockmarket crash. It was a bad decision by their New York agent (reputedly a Polish aristocrat) who poured good money after bad to create a debt Bourke Schiff could not meet.

Then comes the good part of the story, as well as I can piece it together. George's new partners were two Germans, Otto and Ernst, originally from Hamburg, recently naturalized British. They were nephews of Jacob Schiff, a giant among Jewish financiers of New York and frequently a business partner of Sir Ernest Cassel. The Schiff family came to the aid of their London relations and saved the day. Their trust was deserved. All the monies lent were in due course repaid.

The only record I have of all this is what my mother told me and the draft of the letter my grandfather wrote to Otto, explaining the circumstances, thanking the Schiffs and undertaking to respect their generosity.

The draft is attached.

Draft George letter to Otto

(1930?)

My dear Otto

L (Lord Limerick?) has suggested it would be very desirable in order to assist you in your conversation with Mr M (Mortimer?) Schiff that each of us wrote out a statement of our own personal affairs. I welcomed the suggestion and sincerely hope the following facts will prove helpful to you and give some encouragement to believe that whatever further financial assistance you secure for the firm will be for my part honourably and loyally recognized.

I fully understand and appreciate that MS desires to know what has become of the large profits made for the partners during the years of 1927- 1928- 1929. Whilst I am very distraught over the events of the last few months I have an easy conscience when I am asked to give you my own figures – and I hope they will help to explain why I am not in a position to render more financial assistance in the present crisis.

The following figures are abstracts from the private ledger....

(It is relevant to point out that during 1929/30 I had in proportion to my percentage a larger amount of capital in the business than any other partner)

With regard to S/tax allocations in 1929 I put more to the account than actually advised, with the deliberate intention of setting up an "internal reserve".

I have just over £1000 standing to my credit in the "House" ledger.

With regard to my personal affairs you yourself have known for some years the general standard of living to which we have conformed.

My wife and Elaine had until just recently about £9000 between them, some part of which was accumulated in small amounts over a period. I have raised a bank loan of £3000. Part of the remaining £6000 is represented by "odd lots". I have life policies of £1700.

These two sums together are the only assets left to us if anything happened to prevent me from earning a living. We have no other investments whatever. Other than those recorded in the Book of the Firm

You will remember in the summer of 1929 I advised my son Reggie to come home from China. At that time I promised to allow him £50 monthly. The decision was prompted by the ailments of his two children and the gloomy view he took of the outlook in China. That time I promised him £50 p.m. until such time as he could dig himself in here. He arrived over here with about £10,000, £1500 of which I had given him for the purchase of shares the present value of which is £1500. This amount he has willingly returned to me. His membership cost £2000, He is at present with … on probation on £20 per month. His wife has no allowance and no expectations.

He has meantime taken a furnished house for one year @ 4½ gns per week.

I have one sister who has an income of £120 per annum. In 1928 I had a very uneasy mind that such a near relative of mine should be living on such a low standard of life. At my request she took a small house on a 2 year agreement and I promised to supplement her income. Together I obligated myself to the extent of £170 p.a. But I have just recently received a letter from her asking me not to worry myself about her affairs as she felt she would have no difficulty in letting half the house.

I have nothing further to add except I avail myself of the opportunity to ask you to convey to MS and Mr Felix Warburg my very deep sense of gratitude for the magnanimous way they have come to our assistance in the catastrophe which has overtaken the firm

George No date.

The Proposal Letters

In 1931 Russell followed Elaine back to England. He proposed. On 2nd July 1931 he wrote to her mother explaining his intentions and asking for her approval – see the proposal letter attached.

The letter was addressed to "My dear Mrs Greensmith" It begins "I expect Elaine has already told you of what passed between us this week. I may have proceeded in an unorthodox manner, but I wished to find out Elaine's views on marriage, of which I had no previous indication, before approaching you".

In the body of the letter, making his case, he says "I am a very ordinary individual of thirty four summers, trained in my youth to fear God and respect work. My father, who died during the war, managed from literally no beginning to educate a family of five and have mother comfortably provided for. My little mother, who of course in my opinion is the first lady in the land, comes from good Angus and border families. Her only weakness, as far as I can see, is that she spoils her youngest son very badly".

On 4th July he wrote a similar letter to Elaine's father giving full details of his financial position.

On 6th July George Greensmith replies from 155 Sloane Street.

"Let me say at once how very much I appreciate the frankness of your letters to both my wife and myself.

Under the circumstances I am quite naturally interested to know your financial position and prospects, although Reggie had already assured me on that score I could have an easy mind – and your letter and statement is particularly welcomed, and entirely satisfactory.

I do think that both of you are to be warmly congratulated."

Notice of the engagement was given in the Times of London on 15th July 1931 and in the Dundee Courier on 16 July.

Prior to the marriage Russell disappeared up to Scotland. Nothing was heard until a telegram arrived on 11th August. It is postmarked Doncaster and read:

"Miss Greensmith 155 Sloane Street Ldn

Primitive long armed body observed here hurtling south expected arrive about five advise reception committee adopt friendly attitude"

Rusty and Elaine were married on October 14th 1931 at St Michael's Church, Chester Square.

Rusty's letter from Panmure Cottage, Montrose, 2 July 1931 to Mrs Greensmith.

My dear Mrs Greensmith,

I expect Elaine has already told you of what passed between us this week.

I may have proceeded in an unorthodox manner but I wished to find out Elaine's views on marriage, of which I had no previous indication, before approaching you.

Since I first met her I have had the utmost regard for Elaine, which with the passage of time has developed into something stronger and deeper. Now I have screwed my courage to sticking point and wish to ask if I can have the honour of becoming your son in law.

I am afraid I am a very ordinary individual of thirty four summers, trained in my youth to fear God and respect work. My father who died during the war, managed from literally no beginning to educate a family of five and leave mother comfortably provided for. My little mother, who of course in my opinion is the first lady in the land, comes from good Angus and border families. Her only weakness so far as I can see is that she spoils her youngest son very badly.

I have been blessed with a large and healthy body which I have so far succeeded in keeping clean and fit and free of disease. To substantiate this I am to be thoroughly overhauled by a doctor this week – if one lung is reported missing I shall report the fact.

I hope you wont mind my going into all these details but I think it is right that you should know as much as possible before considering my eligibility as a suitor.

I am writing to Mr Greensmith in order to submit details of my finances. In my own mind I am satisfied that I can keep Elaine comfortably, and am prepared to make any sacrifices that may be necessary to that end. As a bachelor one acquires many little selfish habits and I feel that if I don't marry now I shall, although perhaps more wealthy in worldly goods, be quite impossible in four years from now.

I really feel rather an interloper crashing in like this and asking for permission to carry off Elaine. It is needless I think to assure you that it will be my chief aim to look after her and make her happy

There, I cant think of anything more to say to strengthen my case or justify my boldness, Never having gone through this experience before I admit I feel thoroughly gauche.

It is my sincere hope that you will forgive me for creating this domestic disturbance and permit me to be the happiest man on leave.

Rusty.

HRF letter from Panmure Cottage, Montrose, 4 July 1931, to GG

Dear Mr Greensmith,

You have doubtless been apprised of the fact that the young man who kept you awake for two evenings this week, has been bold enough to propose marriage to your daughter. I have refrained for a long time from expressing my intentions but I now feel that the acquisition of wealth is not the only thing to live for, and that if I don't act quickly I'll drift into aged bachelorhood and be a regular old bore.

I have drafted a schedule showing roughly my worth in terms of money, not a very brilliant showing but considering that I arrived in Hong Kong eight years ago with £30 in my pocket it might be a whole lot worse.

I have one quarter share of the firm of Linstead and Davis. My interest brought me in $20,000 last year – not a very bright year. We have managed to increase our fees by about $15,000 which should help current year's results.

Our senior partner CB Brown intends to retire in 1934 when of course my share in the firm will be greater with corresponding in revenue.

I am quite sure that I can economise in many little ways in order to ensure that Elaine will be comfortable and happy. I mean to send her home as frequently as I can, unless of course she objects and then of course I have no say in the matter.

I hope you will agree that my position and prospects warrant my breaking out into marriage and that you will approve rather than damn my audacity.

Yours very sincerely,

Rusty Forsyth

(Schedule of investments etc attached)

George letter from 155 Sloane Street, SW1 of 6 July 1931 to Rusty

My dear Rusty,

Many thanks for your letter. Of course the news had already been broken to us. Let me say at once how very much I appreciate the frankness of your letters to my wife and myself.

Under the circumstance I am naturally interested to know your financial position and prospects, - although Reggie had already assured me on that score I could have an easy mind – and your letter and statement is particularly welcomed, and entirely satisfactory.

I do think that both of you are to be warmly congratulated. Quite naturally I can speak with more conviction about Elaine. She has a most lovable and happy disposition and not in the least bit spoilt by her rambles abroad; and she has the capacity to adapt herself cheerfully to any circumstances in which she might find herself'

She will have a little capital left!! Which should provide her with "pin" money'

Elaine seems to be supremely happy –which gives us both great joy. We are all looking forward to seeing you in a few days time and one evening if Elaine can spare you we will have a" bite" at the club.

Cheerio and the best of luck.

Yours ever

Geo Greensmith

The Engagement

Rusty telegram 11.8.1931 to MEF

Telegram Sloane Square Office stamp. 11 August 1931 From Doncaster

To: Miss Greensmith 155 Sloane Streeet Ldn

"Primitive long armed body observed here hurtling South Expected arrive about five Advise reception committee adopt friendly attitude"

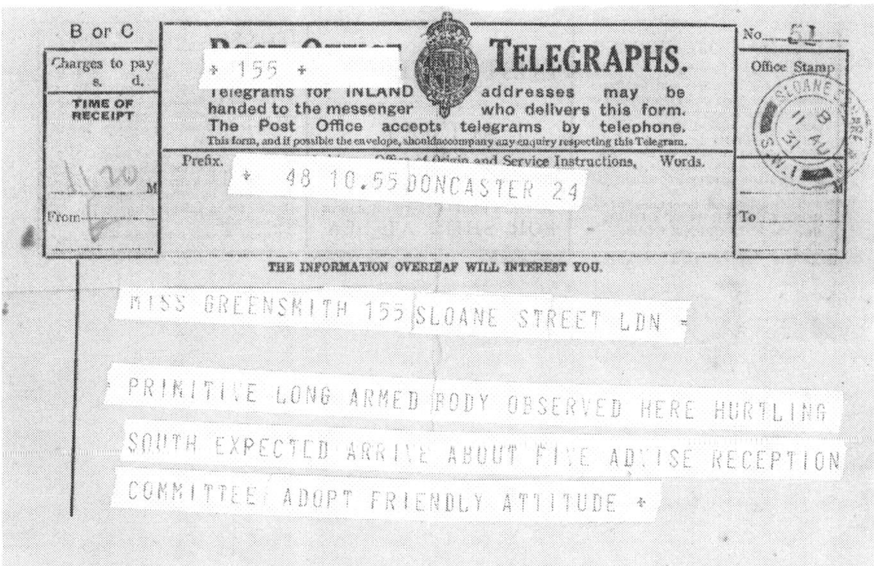
B or C

Charges to pay s. d.

TIME OF RECEIPT

TELEGRAPHS.

+ 155 +

Telegrams for INLAND addresses may be handed to the messenger who delivers this form. The Post Office accepts telegrams by telephone.

This form, and if possible the envelope, should accompany any enquiry respecting this Telegram.

No. 51

Office Stamp

SLOANE SQUARE 11 AU 31 S.W.1

Prefix. Office of Origin and Service Instructions. Words.

+ 48 10.55 DONCASTER 24

From To

THE INFORMATION OVERLEAF WILL INTEREST YOU.

MISS GREENSMITH 155 SLOANE STREET LDN =

PRIMITIVE LONG ARMED BODY OBSERVED HERE HURTLING SOUTH EXPECTED ARRIVE ABOUT FIVE ADVISE RECEPTION COMMITTEE ADOPT FRIENDLY ATTITUDE +

Letter from Ernst and Betty Schiff to Elaine 8 October 1931

(Ernst, nephew of Jacob, wife Betty, daughter of Harold Levy of Sidney)

From Kurhaus Hoven

Freiburg im Breisgau

My dear Elaine,

For years I have been hoping for and looking forward to the day when great happiness may come to you. Now that the day is at hand I shall not be there to witness that joyful day. I am greatly disappointed. Elaine, I do hope you will be very very happy, you deserve to be. You have always been so unselfish, a devoted sister and daughter, and tried to bring cheer and happiness wherever you could. Please give all nice messages to your fiancé and tell him how very sorry we are not to have met him. Don't trouble to answer this note. I only wanted to assure you of the warmth of our feelings for you and of our wishes for your future happiness.

With love from Betty and

Yours very sincerely

Ernst

Telefon 2701

KURHAUS HOVEN
FREIBURG IM BREISGAU

October 8th 1931

My Dear Elaine,

For years I have been hoping for and looking forward to the day when great happiness may come to you. Now that the day is at hand I shall not be there to witness that joyful day. I am greatly disappointed. Elaine, I do hope you will be very very happy, you deserve to be. You have always been so unselfish, a devoted sister and daughter, and tried to bring cheer and happiness wherever you could. Please give all nice messages to your fiancé and tell him how very sorry

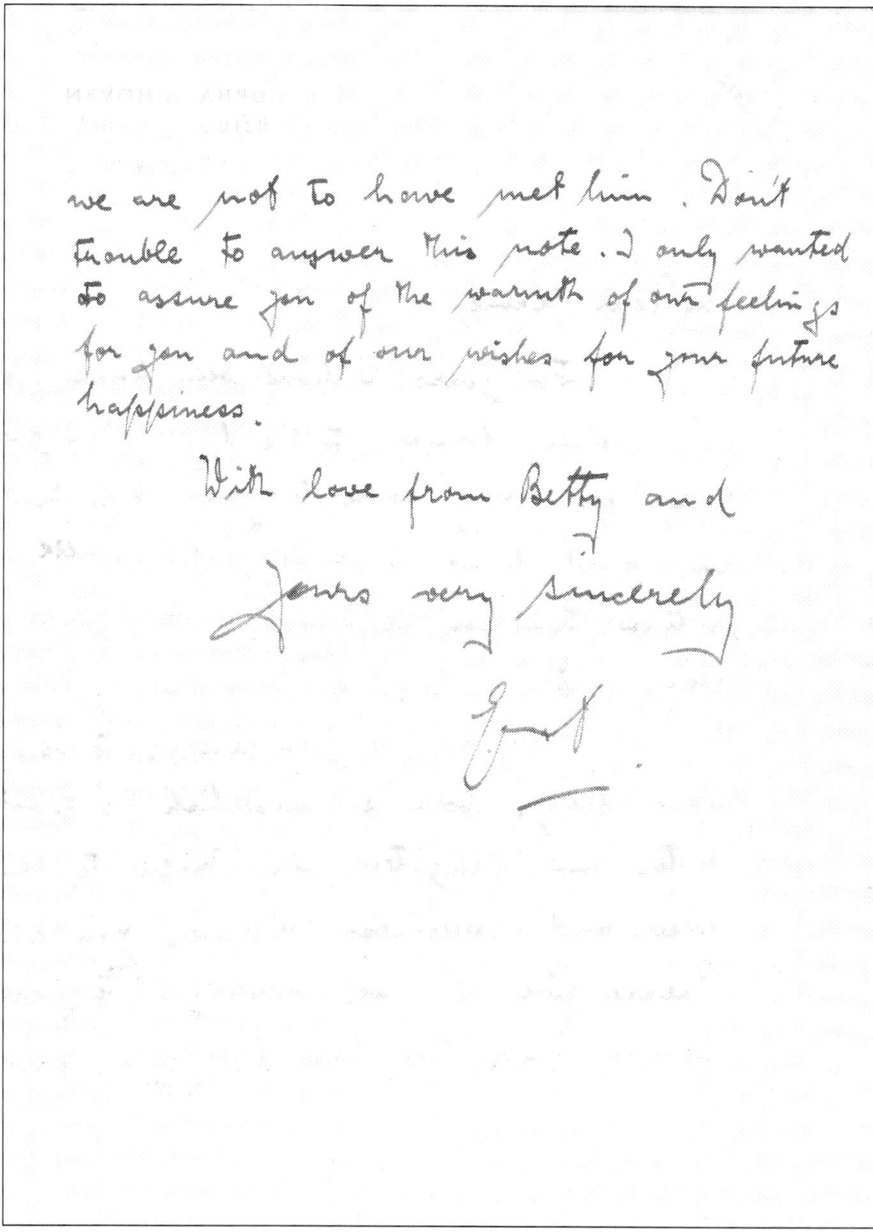
we are not to have met him. Don't trouble to answer this note. I only wanted to assure you of the warmth of our feelings for you and of our wishes for your future happiness.

With love from Betty and

Yours very sincerely

Ernst

Letter from Ernst and Betty Schiff to MEF 8 October 1931

Honeymoon, a day aboard the Koblenz, 18.11 1931

Norddeutscher Lloyd Bremen

My darlings,

I have thought of you very often and wondered how you are getting on, it will be a long time before I get any news from you. Thankyou ever so much for the telegram which we found waiting for us on the ship. As it turned out you could have sent it quite two days later, because we did not finally sail till Saturday afternoon, the 14th! Friday the day after I wrote you I think turned out a pouring wet day and they couldn't load any cargo or get on much with the coaling so that delayed us. Consequently the Hector (Blue Funnel) which we were hoping to catch at Singapore passed us yesterday. Rusty wired to the Ritchies who are on board it saying "Steady on Segrave hope to see you xmas" They replied saying step on it but they must be going about 15-16 knots and our maximum speed is 12! But the Koblenz is amazingly steady, you can hardly believe you are on a ship, there is no vibration and hardly a fraction of movement.

Well we came on board on Friday morning as she was in, had lunch on board and unpacked, in fact we stayed on for the rest of the day as there was not much point in going ashore as it was raining so (That's a fib, we did go ashore for an hour or so, I remember now) We were then supposed to sail early on Sat but as I say we didn't eventually leave until the afternoon. We have a very nice cabin on the promenade deck on port side and we have settled into it very well. The black cat is over the washstand, and we have covered over my cabin trunk with the travelling rug and made a nice seat of it

I must say the service is excellent. Our steward is v nice. He has lent me his iron and ironing board. The ironing is a bit primitive as the iron is almost as big as the board but it gives me something to do. The food is very good indeed, we are at the Pursers table, he is a funny old thing but nice, very fat and enjoys his food (!) and then there are two Americans commander Vickery and his wife, he is technical adviser to the Manila government (or something like that, he constructs ships,) we are going to pass two he has made in the Suez Canal, dredgers for the Phillipine Islands, they are returning from Danzig as the cheapest tender for the ships came from there – seems so funny going there to make them for the P.I.. They are very nice, have two children on board. I am the only English woman on the boat and she is the only American. There are a very large proportion of dagos, the most amazing mixture of Spaniards who look like Chinese and Phillipinos who look like nothing on earth, a Dutch family with Chinese looking eyes, Germans married to Spaniards and so on. Of course besides that there are several genuine Germans and Spaniards. There are two Irish RC clergymen, a Scotsman and a Canadian. So we are a real mixed bag!

There is plenty of music, I must say the band (8 stewards, play awfully well) To wake us up they play "Freut euch des Lebens", one of the tunes out of my book. Then they play for ½ hour at tea which is served on deck and again for dinner. Last night they gave a concert in this room. The Damenzimmer (Ladies Room which title however does not deter men – the only other public room is the Smoking Room which likewise does not deter the women and children, of whom there are stacks) the children have their meal quite near our cabin and it's funny to hear them all yelling in their different languages.

We are both very fit. Rusty gets up early for his bath 7 o'clock and he usually goes for a walk round the deck while I dress and we go down to breakfast about 9. Then we walk a bit, and then I do a job or two, either washing or mending or something. Then about 11.30 we play deck tennis with the Vickerys (or once the Scotsman), then at 12.30 they go and have a drink and then lunch. After lunch we read and sleep till 4 when the band plays. After that more walking or tennis, then it gets near bath time again 6pm and then we get ready for dinner at 7 (Band again) After dinner we talk or walk and afterwards Rusty has a drink and then we go to bed. There, that's a fairly typical day up to the present. The weather is beautiful, not hot. We saw quite a bit of the coast of Italy the first day.

(Rusty is calling)

19th (We were going to play tennis and didn't have time to finish it)

I was going to say we went through the strait of Messina.

We are due in Port Said this evening at 6 pm. I expect we will go ashore although we shall only be there a few hours. Then it will be 5 days I think from there to Djibouti. It is still quite cool.

Last night we passed a sister ship, the Trier, and sent out flares and shouted across to the passengers.

I think this is all the news, we are enjoying ourselves very much.

I hope you are all well and flourishing. I shall so look forward to getting the first news .How is Reggie and Lucy's home getting on? Did the maids like the brooches? I sent a card to Mrs Alexander. I am now going to write to Mithery.

Heaps and heaps of love, my darlings, from kittipuss

Rusty of course sends his love too.

HONGKONG F.C.

15
S. E. KING

11 O. SKINNER — 12 J. A. D. MORRISON — 13 C. B. EASTERBROOK — 14 H. R. CLELAND

9 W. J. CLERK — 10 A. C. I. BOWKER

1 H. R. FORSYTH — 2 J. RALSTON — 3 H. E. D. ADAMS

4 H. H. DAY — 5 J. MILLER

6 V. R. JONES — 7 A. C. GROVES — 8 W. R. ANDREWS

CAPTAIN—H. R. FORSYTH

SHANGHAI R.F.C.

1
G. D. NICHOLL

2 J. SHAW — 3 C. R. W. THOMSON — 4 H. W. P. McMEEKIN — 5 G. F. W. BICHARD

6 R. L. S. WEBB — 7 G. E. GOOLDEN

8 W. E. D. SMITH — 9 E. J. DOWLEY — 10 J. C. STEWART

11 E. A. JENKINSON — 12 B. S. STEPHENSON

13 S. A. GREW — 14 W. D. NEIL — 15 T. LEACH

CAPTAIN—H. W. P. McMEEKIN

Inter Port Rugby – HK FC vs Shanghai RFC

Rusty captained the Hong Kong side. He was later invited to play for Scotland as a "possible"

The defence of the Empire. The Hong Kong Volunteers
Rusty the tallest in the back row

1914 ROLL·OF·HONOUR 1918

Frank Richardson, Captain, 3rd Batts. 24th London Regt. (The Queen's). Killed in action in France, 7th June, 1917.

Ian Kenneth Matheson, Captain, 3rd Seaforth Highlanders. Killed in action in France, Date unknown.

Arthur Noel Joseland, Lieut., Nigerian Regt. Killed in action in East Africa, 22nd September, 1917.

Frederick Henry Robinson, Lieut., 3rd Lincolns. Killed in action in East Africa, 30th September, 1917.

Colin Blomfield Frost, Lieut., Royal Field Artillery. Killed in action in France, 28th July, 1918.

Arthur Francis Deane, 2nd Lieut., Machine Gun Corps. Killed in action in France, 16th August, 1917.

Leonard Joseph Gull, 2nd Lieut., Machine Gun Corps. Killed in action in France, 28th June, 1917.

Alfred Daniel John, Private, London Rifle Brigade. Killed in action in France, 28th June, 1917.

Robert Henry Lloyd, Captain, H.M.T. "Yochow" Lost when "Yochow" was sunk by enemy action in the Mediterranean, 19th March, 1918.

Ernest Arthur Shattock, Chief Officer, H.M.T. "Yochow" Lost when "Yochow" was sunk by enemy action in the Mediterranean, 19th March, 1918.

Neil MacLeod, 2nd Engineer H.M.T. "Yochow" Lost when "Yochow" was sunk by enemy action in the Mediterranean, 19th March, 1918.

Duncan Murray, Chief Engineer, H.M.T. "Hanyang." Died of heat stroke in the Persian Gulf, 10th August, 1918.

Norman Edward Wood, Lieut., R.N.R. Killed in action in the North Sea, 29th July, 1917.

John William Goodrick, 2nd Lieut., I.W.T. R.E. Officer of an hospital ship bound to Mesopotamia; not heard of after passing Malta in April, 1918.

John Francis Summers, Corporal, 4th Battn. Australian Engineers, Mining and Mechanical Co. Killed in action in France, 22nd September, 1917.

Edward J. Mackenzie, Private, 8th Seaforth Highlanders. Killed in action in France, 30th July, 1917.

H. E. Evans, Sergeant, Royal Welsh Fusiliers and Chinese Labour Corps. Died in action in France, 11th January, 1918.

"TAIKOO" EX-SERVICE MEN
HONGKONG.

THIRD ANNUAL DINNER

HELD AT
THE HONGKONG CLUB
NOVEMBER 10TH, 1923

TOASTS

THE KING

THE SILENT TOAST

"TAIKOO"

IN THE CHAIR
D. L. RALPH, Esq.

GUESTS
G. T. M. EDKINS, Esq.
G. M. YOUNG, Esq.
W. NICHOLSON, Esq.

DINNER MENU

Saturday, 10th. November, 1923.

HORS D'OEUVRE

OX TAIL SOUP

GRILLED FISH AND ANCHOVY SAUCE

MINCED STEAK AND POACHED EGGS

ROAST QUAIL

ROAST LEG OF MUTTON AND ONION SAUCE

ROAST POTATOES ARTICHOKES ONIONS

GREENGAGE TART

DESSERT COFFEE

Taikoo ex Servicemen 3rd Annual Dinner Nov 1923, Remembrance Day five years after the war

7

The Thirties

Elaine and Rusty were married in St Michael's, Chester Square, on 14th October 1931. They spent their honeymoon at Peebles Hydro in the Border country. They walked a lot and went on to call on Rusty's elder brother Allan, staying at the Moncreiffe Arms in Bridge-of-Earn, Perthshire.

From there they went on to Genoa where they boarded the SS "Koblenz", – see letter attached. This took them via Sumatra to Singapore. (I have a dinner menu from the Koblenz for Sunday December 6th – "roast goosling " and much more). From Singapore the P&O "Karmala" took them on to Hong Kong which they reached at the very end of December. They then stayed at the Peninsula Hotel, on the Kowloon side, for some months.

Their first home was No.196 Peak Mansions. They changed flats to a bigger flat, no. 18 in the same block after I arrived.

I was born on 23 October 1932. The doctor who delivered me was my parents' friend, Dr Durran, a Scotsman from Perth. I was born, like my brothers, in the Matilda, as the War Memorial Hospital was known.

By this time Rusty was working as junior partner in Linstead and Davis, a local accountancy firm. Over the years he increased his stake to become a full partner.

Soon after I was born, Rusty bought a house, No 298 the Peak. It was a capacious house, with a bedroom for my parents (with ducks flying up the wall), a children's bedroom, with an adjacent bedroom for my Amah, Ah Sim. When I was frightened or couldn't sleep she took me into her bed and I slept like she did with a lacquered wooden block for a pillow.

The house had a large verandah with a fine view across the hills; servants' quarters, for the house boy and Ah Lum the cook, who dealt with the caged turkeys my father received each Christmas, The house had a large garden looked after by a gardener.

My father was much involved with the life of the colony. He acted as accountant to many of the larger enterprises; he was treasurer of the Happy Valley racecourse, an active member of the St Andrew's society; chairman of the rugby club; and later became major commanding the Sottish Company of the Hong Kong Volunteer Defence Corps.

Both my parents enjoyed tennis, golf (at Fanling) and swimming (my first lessons from my father were at Repulse Bay, riding the breakers in my rubber ring). When I was a little older I went to riding school. I won second prize. There were three of us.

In July 1934 my brother Colin Douglas arrived. Our amah wheeled my brother's pram, with me alongside, to Jardine's Lookout. There she sat and chatted with the other amahs. Sometimes the Sikh police, in their khaki shorts, would see Chinese from downtown illegally collecting firewood from the wood along the way. Waving their batons they would chase the Chinese away. We children enjoyed the noise and the chase.

Later that year we returned to England, to show off the two little boys to their family. We went by sea and called in at the French colony of Djibouti. There I was badly scared by a camel, my first surviving memory.

The amah came with us. In Scotland we stayed at the Park Hotel in Montrose. We took her to see the hills behind the town. She shuddered to see the unkempt uncultivated countryside.

1935 was the year of the Royal Jubilee, a year of parades and celebrations.

We returned to Hong Kong on the SS Carthage (15,000 tons – George always recorded tonnage) sailing on 8th November 1935 from the King George Vth dock. George and Lizzie and the amah came with us.

Quotes that follow are from George's cruise diary.

We went first to Southampton to pick up 30 more passengers. On Sunday 10th after rough weather only Rusty and George put in an appearance at breakfast. The amah was "completely knocked over". Heavy rolling in the Bay and only George appeared for lunch on the 10th. George heard the Prince of Wales on the 11th, speaking for Armistice Day. "As many poppies on board as you would see in Throgmorton Street". There was better weather after the Bay.

They called in at Gibraltar and dined at the Rock Hotel, next at Marseilles dining on bouillabaisse at the Restaurant Strasbourg. More passengers and "we now have on board GOC Hong Kong, GOC Singapore GOC India and Governor of Malta". They saw the spot where King Alexander of Yugoslavia and President Barthou of France were assassinated the year before. They took a charabanc to Aix en Provence and had an "excellent lunch at Hotel Vendome". Good weather from there to Sicily and Malta, where two destroyers came out to escort the returning governor and wife. At Port Said George was advised to buy a topee. In the Suez Canal they passed a troopship "with many hundreds of Tommies on board who gave us welcome cheers and cat-calls –"you are going the wrong way!". Reaching the Gulf of Suez all officers and stewards changed into white linen suits. At Aden they visited the ancient Tanks (but no water since 1928), the RAF station and the old town ("squalid beyond description") One impression left in the mind was the beneficent work of the British –water supply, good roads, hospitals, schools, telephone exchange, police "and even a compound for the RSPCA" Subsequently there was a fancy dress ball on board. Quite a few threw cocktail parties before dinner, including ourselves. Many ingeniously thought out costumes… to my astonishment I was awarded the men's prize – as "Farmer Giles". A very merry evening –and far too late to bed." Rusty went as a brigand and Elaine as an American sailor.

They had a three hour tour of Bombay ending at the Taj Hotel for a drink "very much wanted" and dinner.

On November 30th, it being St Andrew's Day, the Scottish contingent on the ship- a pretty large one –met in secret conclave as to how best to celebrate the event in the evening. Our party happens to be seated at the chief officer's table- by coincidence his name happens to be Forsyth – so Rusty figured largely as MC. He threw a big cocktail party before dinner and provided the tartan draped with the Union Jack behind the Commander's chair, also with a bottle of whisky and a Quaich (?) at our table. A piano also had been brought into the dining salon- secretly – and soon after the meal had started the various officers marched in in single file with comical musical instruments, the last of the file- the Purser- bearing the Haggis high above his head. It was some little time before we got the whole company enthused. Many scotch airs were played and sung – the whisky and the Quaich were passed round and towards the end everybody- the commander and even the staid old generals- were on their feet joining hands to the singing of Auld Lang Syne. A very amusing evening, which went with a bang, largely due to the efforts of the first officer's table!"

In Colombo, they hired a car for the day and visited Kandy "one of the most beautiful cities in the East". In Penang they again hired a car for the day and toured the island. At Singapore there was a great to do, officers aboard to greet Major General Dobbie, the new GOC Malaya. They dined by moonlight at the Raffles Hotel. Next day they took on board Sir Andrew Caldecott, the Colonial Secretary who was taking over in Hong Kong. The leavers were escorted out by destroyers Diamond and Duncan "and a squadron of airplanes".

After a rough passage they reached Hong Kong on 12th December" Friends came to welcome back Rusty and Elaine. They took taxis up to 298 The Peak, about 1250 feet above sea level, and "much appreciated fires in all the rooms which surprised us by their spaciousness". Drinks, lunches, dinners at the Hong Kong club, where they were introduced to the Secretary and made temporary members. The grandparents spent Christmas Day, and most of their time in Hong Kong, with Rusty and Elaine and the children. They planned to go back to London by the Pacific route, going East and travelling across the United States.

On 4th January they left for Canton and visited the Sun Yat Sen memorial. They continued to Shanghai and were met by Lizzie's nephew, Noel Bryson, at that time with the Imperial Tobacco Company in China. Next was Japan – Kobe and Kyoto Tokyo and Yokohama (where they saw the Union Jack lowered to mark the death of George Vth). Sailing away in the Empress of Japan (a cut above the Carthage) they saw the last of Mount Fuji in a glorious sunset. They reached Honolulu on 27th January. There was a silver band in white uniforms to greet them. They motored round the island, passing Pearl Harbour, America's most important naval base (there are 15000 troops on the island). On to Waikiki Beach and lunch at the Royal Hawaiian Hotel. "Sailed at 4pm with hundreds of paper streamers connecting ship to jetty. Most of us had garlands round our necks"

On 1st Febuary they docked at Victoria, British Columbia, passed through Canadian immigration controls, drove to the Empress Hotel and hired a car. They went by boat to Seattle and then two nights by train to San Francisco.

It was a beautiful morning but George's camera was locked in his bag so he could not take photos of the Golden Gate bridge, under construction." It is, or will be, one of the wonders of the world". They had a welcome bath and change at the St Francis Hotel and then spent two days touring the town and surrounds -the Redwoods and Stanford University. On the 5th of February they were up early to catch the Daylight Coast Line Express to Los Angeles. They were met by the CPR representative who had booked them into the Biltmore Hotel "How the CPR shepherd us!" Hollywood frankly disappointing, but Beverley Hills on the other hand is the finest residential district we have ever seen. Amongst many outstanding homes was "Shirley Temple's -Americas little sweetheart-with her large dolls house in the garden". On 8th February they went by overnight train to the Grand Canyon "the most impressive sight we have seen – no photo or artist can do it justice" On the 11th they woke up in Kansas "countryside covered with snow and rivers frozen over". In Chicago the CPR representative escorted them to the Palmer House Hotel – a huge place 2300 rooms, each with bathroom. "We passed through Topeka yesterday just about the time they were laying ex Vice President Curtis in his last resting place".

It was very cold. Lunch in the Armours Stockyard canteen. Receipts of cattle for today were 18000 hogs 8000 cattle 10,000 sheep. Next day they had breakfast at the Prospect Hotel, Niagara – "farther down river is a huge Ice Block – the largest in memory"

They arrived in New York on Saturday 15th February, two weeks after they set out from British Columbia. "Drove to Waldorf Astoria for a bath, change and breakfast" On Monday "Took taxi down to Kuhn Loeb, Wall Street, where there was a fair amount of correspondence awaiting me". It was bitterly cold on the Tuesday. On Wednesday George took the subway to Wall Street and called at the Kuhn Loeb office. There he saw Freddie Warburg, John Schiff, Sir W. Wiseman (a sort of British Treasury spy) and Gilbert Kahn. He had an appointment at the Stock Exchange at noon and met up with Lizzie afterwards. She had taken shelter in Trinity church and turned up "frozen stiff". They lunched in Broadway, then walked over Brooklyn Bridge and were nearly frost bitten. On Thursday they took a coach tour and our guide pointed out the various mansions of the "millionaires" – Carnegie's, Rockerfeller's,

Vanderbilts, Otto Kahn, Felix Warburg, Mrs Schiff, Frick, Gould, Hutton etc.

"Friday. Spent day in wall Street district, leaving Jack (Lizzie) to find entertainment at the Frick museum. Picked up cable from Otto Schiff... and discussed the answer with Meyer and Feldman at KLs. Later called on Geo. Maybach (Hallgartens) who took me over and showed me the Stock Exchange. Called HS and Shanghai Bank to cash some money, lunched in Broadway. Call on R. Isaacs (Halle & S) a long talk with him and young Halle and then to KL's office to frame cable reply to Otto."

On Sunday 26th they boarded the Aquitania. The hotel manager sent a Bon Voyage telegram. They sailed at noon, visibility poor. They had a very nice state room and were comfortable. "There was not a tremor and we might have been at the Savoy" Movie, "in Person" featuring Ginger Rogers.

Friday. Beautiful sunny morning. Read Lloyd George's book on the war.

Saturday. Douglas Fairbanks on board and two jockeys coming over to race in the Grand National

Sunday March 1st. "Attended service at 11am and after lunch we all listened to the King's speech, which came through very wel!."

Tueday. Dropped anchor Cherbourg at 8.20 am. "To my astonishment and pleasure saw Reggie and Lucy on board. They had spent the weekend in Paris and came up to Cherbourg to welcome us back. We all had breakfast together. We broke a bottle at 12 o'clock, docked at 3pm and arrived at Waterloo at 6.15." Billy Porter was there to greet them.

They had been away since 8th November the previous year 1935

In October 1936 my number three brother arrived, Murray Greensmith. His birth was announced at a dinner of the Volunteers and Rusty was carried round the tables shoulder high.

Throughout the 1920s and 1930s there was constant trouble on the mainland of China -Nationalists versus Communists and later Japanese. The Japanese invaded Manchuria in 1931. Mao's Long March, the Communist retreat, lasted from 1934 to1935. In December 1937 came the second Sino-Japanese war, marked by the capture of the Chinese capital city, Nanking, and the notorious Nanking massacres. Thereafter the Chinese fought back with some success. But throughout the 1930s there was doubt and nervousness about what the Japanese might do next.

In the background the Germans also were active. Before the 1914 war their only presence in China was the peninsula of Kiaochau, where they succeeded in 1898 to secure a 99 year lease and then proceeded to build up a colonial presence. Tsingtao, the principal city of the colony, was the home port of the German East Asiatic Squadron. It was from here in 1914 that the German raider, the Emden, set out to do immense damage to Allied shipping in the Indian Ocean. In November 1914 an Anglo-Japanese force seized the colony and the Australian cruiser Sydney destroyed the Emden. After the war, despite Chinese lobbying, the territory was assigned, under the terms of the Versailles Treaty to Japan. China did not sign the Treaty but later in 1921 a separate German-Chinese Peace Treaty was concluded.

Under the terms of the Versailles Treaty Germany was prohibited from making alliances with other nations, so there was controversy from the start about the sending of a German military mission to China

However although disarmed, Germany retained a massive armaments industry, but had lost its pre-war markets. It was looking for new markets, in Argentina for example, Soviet Russia, and China.

Sun Yat Sen had visited Germany before the war and made a number of influential contacts. These contacts were renewed after the war and as a result German help was sought to build up the Nationalist army.

From March 1935 the head of the German Military Mission, replacing his predecessor von Seekt, was General Alexander von Falkenhausen. He had been Governor of Belgium in the 1914 war. One of his officers in China was Oskar von Boddien, who from time to time took his leave in Hong Kong and became a good friend of my parents, and in due course my Uncle Oscar. My mother was happy to have an oportunity to talk German and talk about Germany. My father and Oskar had both fought in the 1914 war and had much to discuss.

In 1938 Germany decided Japan would be a better ally than China and the military mission was recalled. Meantime through my parents Oskar had met Dorothy Frost, sister of the Shell chief in Hong Kong. My father had been Dick Frost's best man at Dick's wedding. Oskar took Dorothy back to Germany and they married. She spoke no German but she managed, as she explained in a letter to my mother; " dinner parties were the worst thing!"

We stayed with them in Berlin in May 1939. Dorothy stayed in Germany throughout the war and was well treated – although Oskar her husband was killed in the Crimea, in 1942. His funeral, the coffin draped with the Nazi flag, was presided over by Field Marshal von Manstein. Oskar was posthumously promoted to Colonel and awarded the Knight's Iron Cross with Oakleaves, for bravery in action. He is remembered in his hometown of Neuruppen. His medals are in the military museum in Leipzig

In 1937 George and Lizzie went on another cruise. They left Southampton on 4th September on the Strathmore (23,500 tons), heading for the Mediterranean. There was a service on board to celebrate 100 years of the P&O. They went by Gibraltar and Malta, on to Athens and then the Dardanelles, where they saw dug-outs and trenches and the destruction left by the fighting 20 years before. Next was Rhodes and then Catania and Taormina in Sicily. They reached Naples on the day of the feast of San Gennaro, the patron saint of the city and joined the crowd at the cathedral. Back north towards England, passing an Italian hospital ship bringing wounded back from the war in Spain. Then Gibraltar, Cape Finisterre, Ushant and Tilbury, which they reached on September 25th 1937

In 1938 my mother took me on holiday to what was then French Indochina. We went by boat to Hanoi, in the Red River delta. From there we took a speedy modern train Northward, across the flat rice-growing plains, to the mountains on the Chinese border. Our destination was Chapa (now Sapa), a hill station for the Colonial French and an outpost of the French Foreign Legion. The town was celebrating a recent success in the Legion's ongoing battle with what were then known as bandits, later Nationalists, then Communists.

My mother and I went on pony rides through the woods, led by a local guide. I learnt the French for orange juice and I leapt about in the hotel bedding. It was the only time I travelled alone with my mother.

At the very end of the year, on the 31st December, George and Lizzie set out from Tilbury on the Durban Castle (17,000 tons), on its maiden voyage. George played bridge, Lizzie worked on her tapestry. There were deck sports, cocktail parties and a fancy dress ball, George making another appearance as "Farmer Giles". They reached Lobito on the 13th. There was an unusually large cargo to unload -10,000 steel railway sleepers for the Belgian Congo. George arranged a hire car to take his party to Benguela --- 35 miles there and back.

Construction of the Benguela railway began in 1902, to link the Atlantic port of Lobito in Angola to the Belgian Congo border, and beyond to the copper mines of Katanga, and potentially to Northern Rhodesia. For much of its life it was principally owned by Tanganyika Concessions – "Tanks" on the London stock market, and no doubt of interest to George.

They berthed at Capetown on the 18th and checked in to the Mount Nelson Hotel. They spent some days visiting the sights – the Rhodes Monument – and George lunched with the local directors of Standard Bank. They motored to Groote Schur, the house Rhodes left to South Africa to be the official residence of future Prime Ministers of the Union.

We, the Hong Kong family, were due for leave in 1939. Rather than return to England by sea, as before, my mother was keen to do things differently and try the Trans Siberian route. This had been opened in 1916 and had been used by one side or another during the years of the Russian Revolution.

My mother made comprehensive preparations – books, children's toys, bags of oranges, everything to sustain three young children on a long train journey.

My father had his Passport stamped with a big black swastika by the German consul in Hong Kong. I showed it at the immigration desk when I was next in Germany in 2014. I said this was the last time I was in Berlin. The passport official laughed.

The first stage of the journey was by ship from Hong Kong to Shanghai. The ship was a Japanese ship, the Chosen Maru. It called on several ports on the way North. At one of the ports we took on board a senior Japanese officer. The shore was crowded with Japanese soldiers, waving the Rising Sun flag. The officer saluted them from the ship's deck. On either side of his polished leather boots were two small British boys, my brother Colin and I, in shorts and Clark's sandals. Somewhere no doubt there is a photographic record of the scene. My mother told me the officer was General Tojo, at the time a senior general and Vice Minister of War, possibly saying farewell to one of the Japanese armies fighting at the time in Southern China. He was hanged for war crimes in 1948.

As we approached Shanghai a Japanese destroyer passed us. We dipped flags. They dipped flags. I was standing at the ship's rail next to my father.

He said those are the ships that in the last war escorted our Indian troops to France.

On shore we crossed the bridge to the foreign quarter. It was guarded by Japanese soldiers with their bayonets fixed.

We stayed with friends in Shanghai. One thing my mother had forgotten to bring for the Transiberian stretch was a chamber pot. Our friends made good.

From there we went North by train to Harbin in Manchuria.

In Harbin we stayed with other friends, I have only two memories. First, they had a luxurious deep bath sunk into the bathroom floor. Second, we children knew our host as Uncle Porky and were told he ate bananas with their skins on.

Next came a tramp across an extensive railway yard. We left our Chinese train behind and climbed aboard the Trans Siberian Express. Then we were seven or eight days travelling across Russia. At Omsk the foreigners left their carriage to stretch their legs. The train started to move. It was a scramble for the last of the men to get aboard.

We children teamed up with a Dutch family in the same foreigner's carriage. We stared out of the windows as the forest came close and slid away, hoping always for the glimpse of a wolf or a bear.

In Moscow we dined out at a smart restaurant and Murray distinguished himself by dramatically smashing a wine glass before my mother, laughing, could stop him.

At the border there was nothing to buy except glossy postcards of Karl Marx and pretty little dolls in peasant costume.

In Warsaw station I first saw Polish army officers in their distinctive four cornered hats.

On 19 May we crossed into Germany. We stayed in Berlin with my parents' friends, the von Boddiens. They took us to the zoo (I was frightened because the tigers didn't have cages) and to lunch. My father and the waiter had both served in the war and talked about their respective experiences.

The streets of Berlin were lined with flags. Count Ciano, Mussolini's son in law and Foreign Minister of Italy, was expected and that week signed with

Hitler the Pact of Steel, binding the two nations together, in what became the Axis.

War was in the air.

We went by train to Calais and crossed by the boat-train to Dover. In the restaurant car I had my first and only meal alone with my father. The pudding was apple charlotte.

We were met at Waterloo by my grandparents, with great rejoicing. We went on to stay at the Castle Towers Hotel (long since gone) at Wimbledon Parkside.

In Montrose we stayed at the Park Hotel. We went picknicking on the wind swept North sea beaches, beyond the Links. But I was not excused schooling. I walked each day to a school in a terrace house not far from the hotel.

We were in Montrose when war was declared, on 3rd September 1939. We received our National Insurance numbers and, for each of us, a gas mask in a cardboard box.

The German Letters

Liesel Schmelz
Metzerstrasse 45
Saarbrücken 10.7.1937

(Translated)

My dear Elaine,

Another year has gone, and I am happy to hear from you again. Meanwhile, you must have had your baby. Both my girlfriends now have children, but sadly I am not allowed to have any more. My husband is often very sad that we dont have a son. Well, I console him in those moments as Lilo will soon join the BDM (Bund Deutscher Mädchen)! In two years. She will be a strong and strict Hitler girl. It is such a shame you and your husband do not want to come and visit Germany. It is so much more beautiful here now. We are all with our "hot hearts" with our Führer, he is remarkable in his achievements – truly a genius.

You too might be reading lots of bad lies about Germany, don't take any notice, the others just don't want to acknowledge how much better off we are now. Once the whole world will recognize the Bolshevik danger they will finally show us more understanding

All things being well, we are planning to go to Japan for the Olympics on a cruise ship called "Strength through Happiness". It is not very expensive.

The common German labourer can now afford to go on holiday thanks to Strength through Happiness holidays. In the autumn we will get a foster child, organized by the Nazi Volkwohlsfahrt. They are going to look after the poor, most importantly through the winter months everyone donates just a little monthly, that's how they get all those pennies together. This way millions (of the poor) are looked after. If you can contribute a little, as were such good companions in Munich, please step up for my fatherland. We are so proud and happy here – even the simple man. Now let's leave politics.

On the 20th July I am going to Garmisch Partenkirchen with my kids for a holiday. My husband will go to a sports therapy congress in Bad Elster and afterwards we will tour Germany in our Mercedes cabriolet. We are possibly going to Thuringen, Eisenbach, Wartburg etc. My husband has a big doctor's surgery (?) and is very well liked. He is a very good man with a decent soul and we do get on tremendously well. And what good father he is, spoiling us all just too much.

Lillo had her tonsils out and she suffers from angina, just like me. Her tonsils went septic, just like mine. Lora is a tiny tot – cheeky but always in good spirits. We spend a lot of time in the garden living very privately as my husband works so much and is exhausted in the evenings We love hunting, we have not caught a deer yet, but suffering from wild boar overload. They create havoc and make such a mess of the fields, costing a fortune.

Miss Osthaus is no longer in England, and I have no idea where she is. She is supposed to be living near Munich. I have not heard anything more from Mrs Borchard. Mr Besenfelder is visitings when here in concert.

So, dear Elaine, be well and please send pictures next time you write. I am so interested in all of you.

Best regards and a strong Heil Hitler,

Your devoted Liesel Schmeiz

PS. It is very interesting what you wrote from your colony. A person in a foreign country, whether German or British, would always feel more strongly for their fatherland from abroad. It is the same for us at the borders. Those days long ago when we voted, those were glorious days. I will never forget them.

Elsa Rau to Elaine

From Utrecht, Holland

11 May 1939

Dearest Elaine,

Your letter was forwarded to me in Utrecht, where I live now with my sister. I have only come here about a fortnight ago for good. In January I was here for a visit and went to England also visiting friends. I telephoned to the house of your parents and was sorry to learn that they were absent for a long time. Now I was terribly pleased to hear from you and would be dreadfully disappointed to miss you in Berlin if I had not the answer to make up for it thoroughly in London. My dear friend in Bristol who has tried hard to get me some kind of a job in England has just written that friends of hers want me to stay with them for a month or more and so I will cross over in a few weeks. Of course I shall see you then although I could not tell now if I can stay in London very long. I have not heard from Miss Alton yet when they meant me to come but surely I shall have time to stay in London for a day before going to Somerset and arriving back I shall see more of you I hope. I am very anxious to meet your husband and get acquainted with the boys and it will be quite thrilling to see you again as mother of such a big family. I am sure you are still ths bright and ever laughing jolly Elaine that I knew and loved in Munich. Meantime my home has not only been broken up but I have also lost my country and this is hard in spite of everything I had to go through there. Now I found a home in my sister's house here but as the room is limited and she being very nervous on one hand, and I myself not being satisfied to put my hands down altogether yet I hope to make myself useful still and as I love England I do hope to be able to stay there a while. I hope to get a visa as I have a permit to live in Holland where my home will be from now.

My sister's eldest daughter is married and lives in Gerards Cross near London, she has four children and many others of my German friends are in England now and spread all over the world.

I shall also send you a little note for Russell, and hope this will reach you in Berlin. Should you stop in Holland on your way home will you send a word? Also if you come to Utrecht on your way to the Channel I should love to meet you at the station.

It is nice to know that we will meet now if all goes well. Lots of love and best wishes and do remember me to your husband.

Yours very sincerely

Elsa Rau

George Letter 2.10.1938 The Munich Scare

Dear Elaine and Rusty,

We have just emerged from an unforgettable week and we have many times wondered about how the various reaction has affected Hong Kong. From the very abyss of depression earlier in the week, when about everyone had abandoned hope came the astounding news of Hitler's last minute invitation to Chamberlain to meet him D.M. in Munich. When the result of the meetings became known all the pent up emotions were released and expression was given to them in the wonderful reception they gave Chamberlain on his return. But you will have already read all about this. The profound feelings of relief were reminiscent of Armistice Day and Mafeking.

The ARP authorities deserve the greatest credit for their foresight and plans, which must have been long since thought out and prepared. As soon as the emergency arose and within a few hours the whole of London was plastered with bills notifying where to apply for gas masks and thousands of people seemed at once available for fitting. Our "station2 was the former furniture shop opposite our front door so we could therefore see the queue all day lined up in good illustration of foresight. Reggie told us that overnight the whole of rhe Brooklands track – a good landmark from the air – was sprayed with green paint as well as the Vickers works on the far side. The most conspicuous signs of being on a war basis are however the parks and open spaces. These all look like huge building yards – heaped up earth and piles of timber. They have not been digging the trenches haphazard – all were carefully pegged out ten days ago but when the word go was given there were thousands at the job– Hyde Park Green Park Battersea Park Kensington Gardens Streatham Tooting in fact everywhere – even the gardens on the right going up Sloane street. Men were working in shifts. As soon as the 10pm shift finished another lot were waiting to work through the night with the aid of flares. Tents and canteens were installed. Lorries with gas filled cylinders, first aid stations and fire fighting appliances.

Many thousands of people left London earlier in the week and cars and buses with luggage were like those preceding Bank Holiday. School children were being evacuated every day, and the children at the school almost opposite to us in Sloane Street left with their bags to some places in the country by Charas on Wednesday. I fancy most of the young have rather enjoyed the excitement. In any case even if geography is not one of their strong points they will remember "Czechoslovakia".

8

1939 – England and back to Hong Kong

In preparation for their return to Hong Kong my parents had been looking for a school for me. They saw several in Scotland. They settled on Ardvreck in Crieff, a red sandstone Victorian pile not far west of Perth. The idea was that I would start boarding there in January 1940, when I was seven, and, for so long as my parents were abroad, I would spend the holidays in Bridge of Earn with my cousins. In due course, at 13, would go on to Glenalmond, a Scottish school on the English public school pattern, a school my father, since his own schooldays, had always respected.

We returned to London and the Castle Towers in Wimbledon. On the war front not much happened. Bren gun carriers rumbled past the hotel. On Parkside the newspaper headlines kept us informed of the tragedy of the submarine Thetis, trapped with all its crew while on trials offshore.

Father smoked Players Navy Cut cigarettes and I eagerly awaited the next packet with the next cigarette card. The series was battleships of the world.

We moved out of London to a house at Barton on Sea in Sussex, lent to us by my mother's old headmistress, Miss Fuller. We looked out on the sea, watched the dolphins sporting along the sea's edge, saw a Fairey Battle fly by, a new fighter bomber, built of wood in Norfolk.

While we were in Barton on Sea, news began to come through on our radio set of a developing naval battle off the mouth of the River Plate, the river which divides Argentina and Uruguay. My father listened intently, crouched before the radio, anxious to hear the outcome. The three English cruisers, Ajax, Exeter and Achilles, trapped the Graf Spee, a brand new battle cruiser, pride of the German fleet, in Montevideo harbour. The Captain scuttled the ship then shot himself in a Buenos Aries hotel bedroom. One of the cruiser captains came later to Ardvreck to tell us all about it.

They were still selling postcards of the German crew of the Graf Spee, a generation later, when I visited Montevideo for a bankers' conference.

I went to school in nearby New Milton. We drove there each day through autumn woods (not seen before). I watched my first Guy Fawkes bonfire, I was put in the school ring for my first and only boxing match. I punched my opponent on the nose and he burst into tears, bleeding. I burst into tears in sympathy.

One day I went back home, full of the news that I could now count up to ten in French. But there was nobody there. I asked at the shops rounds the village green. The green grocer said my mother had been carried off in an ambulance. It transpired she had diphtheria, and was very ill. She took a long time to recover. As a result my father had to postpone his return voyage to his business in Hong Kong. He flew back later with Imperial Airways. My brother Colin and I saw him off from a wind -swept Hampshire railway platform. We presented him with a farewell present of a school pen, probably with spare nibs.

It was the last time I saw him. He flew from Southampton, on December 19th in a flying boat. It landed in Marseilles, Brindisi, Alexandria, Lake Victoria, Calcutta, Rangoon, Bangkok and Singapore. They dined and rested overnight on the water. Reaching Hong Kong he saw the ship he should have caught, entering harbour.

That was at the end of December. Early in January my grandmother took me by train to Ardvreck. My mother had not fully recovered from her bout of diphtheria. My grandmother had taken on the task of assembling all my school kit. It was a long list. A tweed jacket, an eiderdown, a tartan rug, the book of common prayer, at least two copies of the bible, a kilt, a balmoral, a sporran; and everything susceptible marked with a Cash's name tape, with my name and number (78).

Sadly, my grandmother, who was a Christian Scientist for at least part of her life, had marked me down for my school life as an Anglican. This meant that on Sunday mornings, kilted up, the Anglicans were marched off to the local Episcopalian church, much further away than the far better attended Presbyterian Church of Scotland.

In the middle of my first term my mother and two brothers set off from Liverpool for New York and the New York World Fair.

There was a crowd at the dockyard gates, many of them Jewish refugees from Germany. My mother speaking fluent German chatted with several of them. It was a friendly gathering. But when the iron gates were opened the friendly neighbour became a savage competitor. My mother had many dear lifelong Jewish friends, but was aware how single minded they could be when in competition.

From New York they travelled by train to the West coast and sailed on from there in the Empress of Japan to Hong Kong- in the reverse direction of her 1926 trip, returning from Hong Kong. And this time caring for two young children.

She wrote a ditty about their travels, of which I have only a fragment:

"Though we're only five and three,

we've been all around on the Underground, the El and the LNE"

(The El was the New York Elevated Railway.)

They reached Hong Kong and had barely unpacked when the authorities advised that all wives and children of belligerent nationals should leave.

Hong Kong and Australia

A group of Hong Kong friends, wives and children, set sail for the Philippines. From Manila they went North to Baguio; where Colin went briefly to school.

Many of the British wives decided Australia would be preferable and sailed onward in August. The Dutch boat (Rotterdamsche LLoyd) that took them was the TSS Slamat. I have a copy of one of their dinner menus, for August 16th 1940, signed by four of the wives in my mother's group –Elaine, Mary Williams. Doreen Ralph and Katherine Durran (wife of Doctor Durran, from Perth in Scotland, our Hong Kong doctor, a Major like Rusty in the Volunteers)

Elaine took a flat in Sydney (Mason Manor, Birriga Road)

In December I had bad earache at School and was rushed to hospital in Broughty Ferry, close to Dundee. My mother in Australia and my father in

Hong Kong were both distraught. I had a double mastoid operation. I was there in Fernbrae Hospital until February and had to be taught to walk again.

While I was there I was given a banana and was told it would be my last until the end of the war. Too high a cost in merchant shipping. The battle of the Atlantic had begun.

By this time Hitler controlled most of mainland Europe.

Since the beginning of the war German raiders had sporadically attacked the East coast ports of Scotland and one German raider flew past my hospital window.

A lifetime later I was at a smart party on board a yacht in the Pool of London. Another guest was Lord Thomson of Monifieth, a small town along the coast from Broughty Ferry. I said I had spent time at a hospital close by, with ear trouble. Where? Fernbrae, I said. And who was your doctor? Dr Mather, I said. "He was my doctor too. I had a spot of bother with my ears back in 1935…."

He went on to tell me that his first job had been with the D.C. Thomson company of Dundee – although these Thomsons were no relations of his. They were publishers of the Dandy and Beano comics which constantly made fun of Hitler, Goering and Mussolini ("Musso da wop is a big-a-da flop").The Thomsons were worried that the Germans might invade the east of Scotland and they gave the young Lord Thomson travel expenses and sent him off westward to Glasgow to find an alternative site for the Thomson printing presses.

On April 1st 1941 my sister Hilary was born in the War Memorial hospital in Sydney. From her hospital bed my mother wrote a few days later to the family. The first paragraph is all about the war with question marks about what the Japanese might do next. The rest of the letter is cheerful and mostly about the birth and the new baby.

Later in the year Rusty and his good friend Eric Bryden flew down to Australia. I have a certificate from Qantas Empire Airway stating that Mr R. Forsyth "has flown over the Equator in the Empire flying–boat 'Coriolanus'…thus joining the band of progressive travellers who 'cross the line' by air" 6.20 gmt 4th July 1941.

Rusty and Eric were visiting their wives, both of whom had produced a small daughter. There was a joint christening, both mothers looking pleased and plump.

The two fathers, both Scottish accountants and both in the Volunteers, were busy soldiering all year in Hong Kong, keeping fit, inspecting defences, getting to know the lie of the land. Both had a happy time with their families in Australia. My mother told me of the unbelievable amount of oysters she consumed. My father wrote to me often, in his very precise hand, and told me of the gruelling time he and his men had, training in intense heat, and consuming, to rehydrate, an unbelievable number of cups of tea.

From Australia my father flew back to Hong Kong by way of Singapore. While waiting for onward transport he motored north with friends to see something of Malaya.

On October 14th 1941, only weeks before the fighting, he wrote to Elaine, a letter which I treasure (attached).

"To our Good, Kind, Clevaire 'Lainey Greetings! Wheras today 14th October 1941 is the TENTH ANNIVERSARY of our WEDDING DAY I want to assure my wee wifie that those ten years have taught me many things, but chiefly to appreciate how very very fortunate I have been to have a mate like 'Lainey

For my part the attachment grows deeper with the passing of the years and I step out eagerly on the second cycle of ten years with the added happiness and responsibility of having TWO WOMEN to care for – bless 'em
Russ"

My parents were increasingly worried that I had been left on my own in Scotland. Rusty wrote to grandfather George in London, asking if there was any way arrangements could be made for me to travel to Australia, to join my mother, two brothers and sister. He replied saying this would be very difficult. There was a long waiting list for passages across the Atlantic. Furthermore the shipping companies would require that I being a minor would have to be accompanied. And what would happen to me in America? Who would look after me? How would I cross to the west coast and travel on to Australia? In the end George recommended that my parents made use of any contacts they had with Australian and New Zealand shipping lines to see if they might be able to suggest how a passage might be arranged,

But time was running out. Rusty, as commander of the Scottish company of Volunteers led the traditional St Andrew's Day parade to the Union Church in Hong Kong. The photograph of the company, in smart khaki and wearing Glengarries, appeared in the South China Morning Post on the following day, December 1st.

Letter from Elaine to her family

In mid war. 3rd April 1941, from hospital bed in Sydney, Australia, two days after birth of Hilary Mary

My darlings, all at Glenealy, Hardmead, Green Warren and Carnethy, I do hope the flora and fauna is treating you as kindly as Sydney is treating me, although I'm afraid that's wishing too much. The war news certainly looks better these last few days, what with Yugoslavia's coup d'etat and Italy's naval defeat in the Mediterranean. Let's hope our Merchant shipping losses keep low so that you get enough to eat, and now that it's Spring with you the bombing hours should be shorter. Anyhow everyone here thinks you're all wonderful if that's any consolation.

And before I go on to tell you the news about Baby, thank you all more than I can tell for everything you've done for Alastair. I was so delighted when I got my Carnethy-Hardmead cable mentioning that he was "frisky". Then yesterday I got mother's letter of Feb 9th (quite a speed merchant for these days) saying she was just waiting for a letter from Nan saying A was with her so I gather he must have left the home about the beginning of February. I am so hoping he has no after effects, poor little chap. One of the nurses here said it takes about three months to get over a double mastoid. Please tell him his brand new sister sends him a special grunt.

Well, you can imagine how thrilled I was when I heard them say "you've got a fine baby girl" Because of various portents I came in about 8.30am. Mary Bryden was a brick – her poor face was quite scared when she came running up to the flat in response to Nurse's prearranged message. She did the phoning etc, and away we sailed in a taxi. On arrival we made certainly an April Fool of the Sister for she didn't know which was the patient. Well there I stuck, and believe it or not I spent till 5pm embroidering initials on towels and pillowcases for them here: I was just in the middle of a particularly fine M when I felt it was time to down tools, and at 5.50 Hilary, the pet, was here. At first glimpse she was just like Murray and if I take off my coloured spectacles I can see she is no oil painting, but she's fine and sturdy and full of beans. She's dark, a brunette in fact. Her face is more my shape than Rusty's, but I think she has R's hands and nails. She weighed 8 ½ lbs by the way. When March 28th went past I wrote to R and said I am now resigned to being an April Fool, and sure enough that was the day, poor Hilary. They say it doesn't matter after 12 noon. I caused quite a stir at Mason Manor and environs. I must say everyone has been most kind and what a difference it has made having friends around. This is a very nice hospital, no complaints at all. I have a nice room to myself overlooking the grounds which remind me of Castle Towers garden (Colin remarked the same immediately he arrived), the sun shines from morning till night –in fact it's been pretty warm. Some lovely old trees, pigeons cooing and a pheasant strolling around Apparently the main block was a private mansion, which was presented after the last war, by somebody, called Vickery, to Sydney (or to the Methodists, I hear it is a Methodist Hospital) together with two or three surrounding houses, which are now nurses homes. This maternity block is less than five years old: they average 30 to 40 babies and Mothers all the time, so there are about two births a day or more.

The boys and Nurse came along yesterday afternoon – all dressed up in their Sunday best, and well washed and brushed. They are tickled to death, and soon up to their old tricks of wanting to clamber. R was very well and chirpy in his last letter, which I got yesterday. He was just beginning to get anxious and look for cables – actually I sent him a birthday greetings one on the 28th – saying "all well but no news yet" I had five cables and wires on "our" birthday, felt quite festive – also some flowers and scent. And since coming in here have had eight letters and one telegram (local) so you see I am not neglected. Betty Schiff is coming along tomorrow – afraid she is still worried about her Mother.

Doctor just been in: everything all right. I'm getting hungry, and if supper doesn't come soon I shall have to fall back on my last line of defence, liquorice all sorts

Lots and lots of love and hugs to you all –I do hope you, Mitherie, are keeping fit and well, haven't heard for a little while. Hilary sends you all a varied assortment of grunts, finger-suckings and (yes) hiccups

Love from Lainy

The Blitz

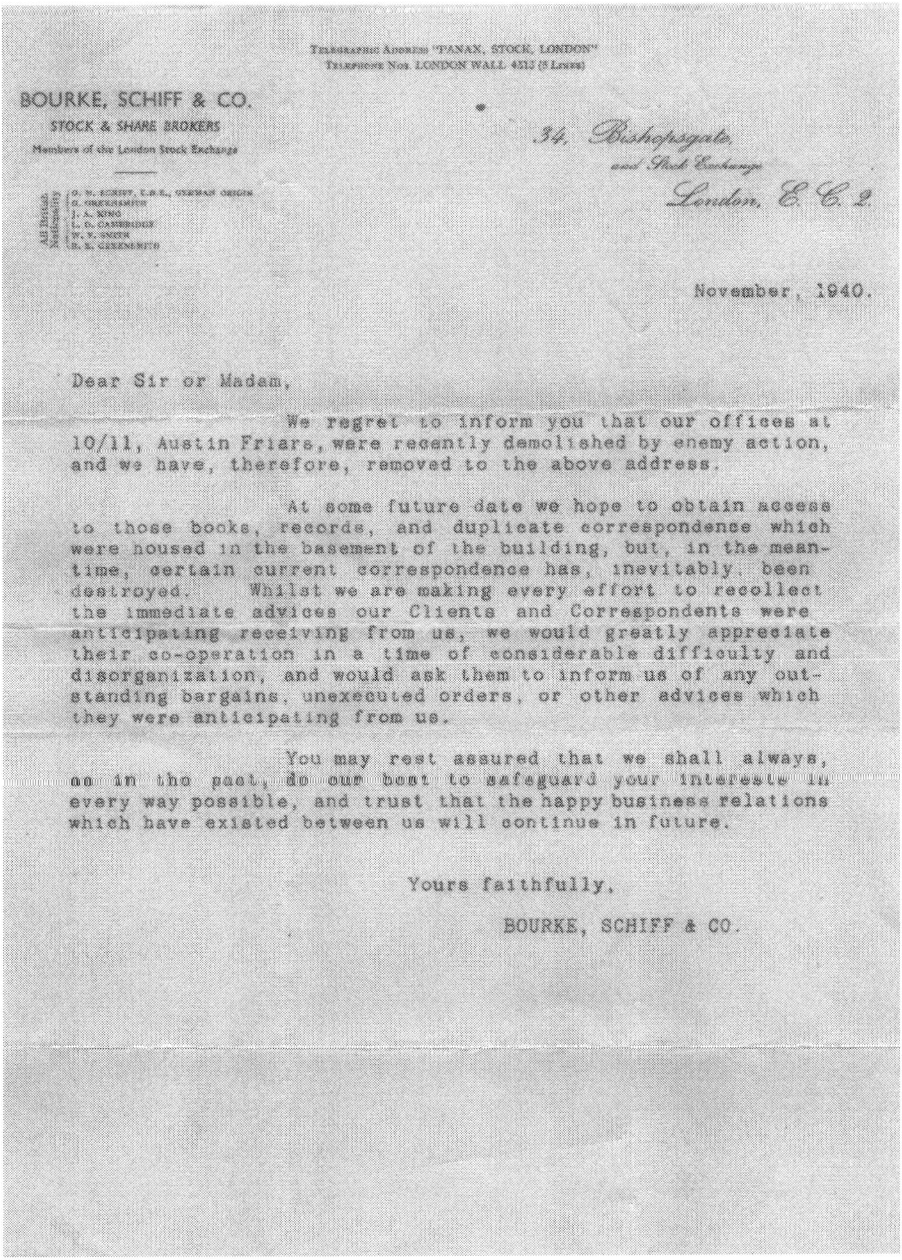

TELEGRAPHIC ADDRESS "PANAX, STOCK, LONDON"
TELEPHONE NOS. LONDON WALL 4513 (5 LINES)

BOURKE, SCHIFF & CO.
STOCK & SHARE BROKERS
Members of the London Stock Exchange

34, Bishopsgate,
and Stock Exchange
London, E.C.2.

November, 1940.

Dear Sir or Madam,

We regret to inform you that our offices at 10/11, Austin Friars, were recently demolished by enemy action, and we have, therefore, removed to the above address.

At some future date we hope to obtain access to those books, records, and duplicate correspondence which were housed in the basement of the building, but, in the meantime, certain current correspondence has, inevitably, been destroyed. Whilst we are making every effort to recollect the immediate advices our Clients and Correspondents were anticipating receiving from us, we would greatly appreciate their co-operation in a time of considerable difficulty and disorganization, and would ask them to inform us of any outstanding bargains, unexecuted orders, or other advices which they were anticipating from us.

You may rest assured that we shall always, as in the past, do our best to safeguard your interests in every way possible, and trust that the happy business relations which have existed between us will continue in future.

Yours faithfully,

BOURKE, SCHIFF & CO.

George letter to Rusty 20 April 1941

From Glenealy, Pembroke Road, Woking.

My dear Rusty,

I do hope you are getting good news of Elaine and the new arrival. It may be you have been able to get down to Sydney before you get this. How thrilled you both must be that it was a girl this time. If she inherits the brains of the parents and the cheerful light hearted disposition of her mother am afraid she will be a spoilt darling. We are enormously looking forward to the letter which will tell us all about it. We had a letter from Nan this week. Although Alastair's progress has been somewhat slow she hopes he will be able to resume school next term. Apparently the operations have left no permanent disability. Am sure Nan has had a very strenuous time as A has a strong will and requires a firm hand – but one can hardly blame the little chap for that.

We are living dangerously here. Have had two vicious raids this week and been bombed blasted and burned. You will have heard from the wireless or the papers some of the damage. So many buildings dear to our heart. Shattered or gutted. The Old Pensioners Hospital at Chelsea. Chelsea Old Parish Church. The City Temple where mother and I were making a habit of going to before we vacated the flat. The West End is a sad sight. Fortunately the flat remains intact although there are quite a number of shattered windows very nearby. In fact there is hardly any street of any size in London or near suburbs that has not some evidence of bomb blast. I had to get to the office the next morning by devious ways. W.loo was closed – by train to Wimbledon then by bus tube and walking. Many streets strewn with broken glass and gutters filled with burnt ashes from various fires – some of which were still smouldering. I really felt quite sad this morning. I went for a walk to meet mother from church. It was a typical English spring morning. Cuckoo – for first time. All the birds twittering, trees, shrubs bursting forth and all the spring flowers at their best. And then I thought of all the shattered homes, sufferings and anxieties of so many thousands of families. On the night of the "Big Raid" I went out into the garden to have a look at the searchlights. There was an incessant hum of planes passing over – intermittent gunfire and could see the shells bursting overhead. I had the grim satisfaction of seeing a blazing enemy plane coming to earth a few miles away. I rushed in to bring mother but by the time she got her coat on it had disappeared. We have had 2 soldiers billeted on us. Fortunately they have been very tidy and very quiet. They leave tomorrow a.m. I expect we shall get two more. The food situation is becoming a bit of a problem. Elaine very thoughtfully suggested sending us an occasional parcel which will now be very welcome. I have paid £14 14/- for Alastair's anaesthetist and £47 5/- for his school fees for next term.

Am afraid we have to go through a very grim and testing time for the next few months. We're making no money in the City but must carry on and hope for the better days to come and that our diminishing capital will see us through and at the end leave us with sufficient to take us both to Sydney -or Hong Kong to see our little darling Hilary. That's something to live for and look forward to.

Cheerio. Dad

Rusty to Elaine 14.10.41 Ten Happy Years

From Linstead & Davis address, Exchange Building, Hong Kong

To our Good, Kind, Clevaire 'Lainey

GREETINGS!

Wheras today 14th October 1941 is the TENTH ANNIVERSARY of our WEDDING DAY

I want to assure my wee wifie that those ten years have taught me many things, but chiefly to appreciate how very very fortunate I have been to have a wife like 'Lainey.

For my part the attachment grows deeper with the passing of the years, and I step out eagerly on the second cycle of ten years with the added and happiness and responsibility of having TWO WOMEN to care for – bless 'em

Russ

The Last Letter - Rusty to Elaine 4.12.1941

Pre Christmas

From Linstead and Davis

Exchange Building, Hong Kong

My darling

At last I have a little peace and quiet – life seems to have been rather hectic since our return from camp. I have been submerged in work, trying to bring it up to date, and on top of that comes church parade, followed by political and military flap and general excitement. Tonight has been most peaceful – I have cleaned up the remnants of a very excellent steak and kidney pie, followed by prunes and am feeling just fine. Just turned off the wireless after listening to Harry Roy and orchestra playing "my heart belongs to daddy" and am now re-reading your last three letters – first of which arrived in camp.

Wish I had been with you all at the zoo. It's a grand spot. And Colin's message about the shark made me laugh – I remember the ugly brute, but I don't remember seeing Murray's toy train. You really want a whole day to do the zoo properly. Your S afternoon excursions with one or both tigers is a good idea – C. is good company and he will be alright when he grows up a bit.

Which reminds me I have done nothing for their Christmas (nor for yours) but sending parcels to Australia is such a business these days and I never seem to have time to do any shopping. Will you please get the tigers (and h. m.) something good for xmas on my behalf.

Now to your most (?...) letter which arrived two days ago. As I suspected you are already counting on Atta's arrival, wheras it may be some considerable time before we get him on the move, so you must not be too disappointed if there is a long delay. I found that Slap (?) had contemplated bringing his daughter out from home and Thomas Cooks in Adelaide (I think) said they could arrange for her to come the long way round. The catch apparently is the route via America – many difficulties and a huge waiting list which corroborates what Daddy said. But I don't feel like sending Atta by the all sea route – at least three months on a blackout ship and many risks. I have wired Daddy that I am prepared to pay the fare of an escort to America but not to take definite action until I wire again. I don't want to have the wee chap stranded in America and that might happen if the Jap eventually runs wild. So I suggest that having sown the seed at home, we mark time for a few weeks until we see how events shape themselves. Sea travel is most uncomfortable just now and I don't feel like asking Atta to rough it on his own.

To swing to Mary Roberts – she must be having a wonderful time with staff changing every week. CC told me he had had a red hot letter choking him for daring to mention parties and efficiency of houseboy and staff. Poor old CC observed that Mary didn't realise that he had the parties thrust on him by BS staff passing through, but he realised it was useless trying to explain. I again regard myself as being most fortunate!

Well now – let's see what local news there is to dispense. This week has been almost exhilarating - the war flap came on Tuesday and rumours were flying all over the place. And then it subsided and again we are almost back to normal. I dined with Jock on Tuesday (after we had attended Ho tung's cocktail party in the Gripps to celebrate his diamond wedding) Jock was furious – he had been warned to stand by to accompany KMG out of the colony in case of trouble! The Japs have certainly got a fright – even the hotel barbers have disappeared – but I am very doubtful about a real showdown coming off. I expect your Aust papers have banner headlines about the Jap situation whereas we are staging a perfectly good race meeting on sat.!

Not that our heads are entirely in the sand. I took an afternoon off on Monday and dragged Eric and ?Prophet round our new positions. We operate with Canadians –from the Gaspe Peninsula – that gets you guessing but I have just looked up the old atlas to make sure of my ground. You'll find it in province of Quebec. They are a keen bunch and we get on well together so far.

I think I mentioned in my last short note that Camp had been very successful. We covered many miles of paddy and gained the reputation of being the fittest coy in camp. It was great fun and we carried out some very good schemes. The weather was changeable but it did not rain- the poor blokes who followed on and are in camp this week are having a wet time – it has rained on and off most of the week.

So swing again – you might tell Mrs Levy that I am in process of packing all our new linen and best blankets to store in the Dairy Farm for the duration. This is in accordance with her advice!

And now by byes – I'm off to bed. Don't worry about the situation or believe half the Sydney papers rubbish. Everything is going to programme. We haven't been too clever in Libia but we ought to have enough weight to carry the operation through to a successful conclusion and in the meantime our old friend Joe Stalin seems to be the king pin. The Russky is doing big business just now and must be giving the Bosche rather a headache. The Caucasus is still a place to watch although it looks as though he may go down through Spain to North Africa. Anyway we must keep our heads and all will be well. Today's great thought is don't panic!

Nightie nightie – goo' night my dear. Hope HM still thrives – I'll have to deal with her later.

All my love – and keep FIT

Russ

9

The Battle for Hong Kong

On 21st June 1942 Hitler invaded Russia. On 27th June Japan signed the tripartite pact with Germany and Italy

My father wrote to me often that year, in his beautifully clear handwriting, telling me of the Volunteers manoeuvres, of the great heat and the number of cups of tea he had consumed.

Most of his letters I kept in a wooden writing case, later lost on a train to Scunthorpe in Lincolnshire. One of the letters in the box was from a member of the Japanese colony in Hong Kong. My father was chairman of the Hong Kong rugby club (he had been a "possible" for Scotland) and the letter asked for his help in teaching rugby to the Japanese. We are small but brave, it said.

Pearl Harbour was attacked on the 7th of December. At 4.45 am on the 8th of December a Japanese-speaking British Army intelligence officer (Charles Boxer) intercepted a call from Japanese headquarters ordering the immediate simultaneous attack on Hong Kong, Malaya, Siam and Indonesia.

My father was at the front line in the New Territories, on the Kowloon side of the colony. The defenders were overwhelmed and withdrew across the harbour to Hong Kong island.

On 9th December Japanese planes sank the British battleships Repulse and Prince of Wales, on the eastern coast of Malaya. This was a shattering blow for Britain and the last hope of reinforcement for Hong Kong

Rusty was in charge of the withdrawal from Kowloon. He left across the harbour on the last Star Ferry, with machine guns blazing over the stern.

The Japanese finally landed on Hong Kong island on 18th December. The landing at the North Point power station was resisted by the Hugheseliers, an elderly group of Volunteers named after their founder. Few survived.

By 23rd December there was little resistance except on the southern tip of the island. My father, commanding B Company, "Scots of all nations", held the line from his command post in the old police station on Stanley Peninsula. The previous day he had taken his men for a swim at the beach on Stanley where he used to take his children to swim. Then he shaved his head and prepared for what lay ahead.

There was a fierce fight on the night of the 23rd, a direct assault on Rusty's position. Two Japanese light tanks were destroyed and a third was driven off. Early on, Rusty was badly wounded. He ordered his Sergeant Major, Tommy Swan, to leave him. Tommy refused. My father said he would be put on a charge for disobeying orders. Tommy still refused.

According to "Second to None, the story of the Hong Kong Volunteers":

"At 1am on Christmas Day, the decision was made to withdraw to the next position. The survivors of the Stanley Platoon and some of the Middlesex men made a dangerous withdrawal …being joined by some survivors of Forsyth's unit. Forsyth himself was too badly wounded to move and so he and Company Sergeant Major T. Swan stayed behind to fight to the finish."

A burying party after the battle found six bodies in the police station. One had the insignia of a major. Two others were most likely Tommy Swan his sergeant major and a former Argyll and Sutherland piper, McKay.

A member of the burying party later told Doctor Durran, in prison camp, that all six had been given a proper burial. It is a haunting thought that the Japanese must finally have broken into the police station

Tommy Swan and my father lie side by side in Stanley Military cemetery.

Civilian survivors at Stanley believe the last stand of the Scots saved them all from a massacre like the notorious massacre at St Stephen's College nearby. The surrender of the colony on Christmas Day may also have helped prevent more killings.

Brigadier Lawson, commander of West Brigade (one of the two into which the island was divided) went missing after its HQ was destroyed. His body was later found in scrub where he had bled to death.

Brigadier Wallis, commander of the East Brigade, drew up in prison camp a list of those he believed deserved an award. Head of the list was Major Forsyth, who he recommended should receive the Victoria Cross, Britain's highest award "For Valour". After the war Colonel Oliver Lindsay, who wrote two books on the battle for Hong Kong, criticized Wallis for failing to support his case. In due course Rusty received a Mention in Despatches for gallantry in the field.

George VI King of England, Emperor of India, wrote to my mother, probably a standard letter, expressing his sympathy for her loss and his thanks to her husband for Rusty's sacrifice in serving the Empire.

Letters from Captain Prophet, Colonel Rose, and Benny Proulx are attached, all of whom knew Rusty well. Prophet and Proulx were with him at Stanley. Rose commanded the Volunteers from before the war.

After the Battle.

There was a long wait for news of what had happened in Hong Kong. Elaine did not learn of Rusty's death until late in January, or possibly early February. It was devastating news, and desperately sad for her parents. Rusty gone, the house gone, the business gone and Elaine alone on the other side of the world with three children, 7 and 5 and scarcely one.

I was told the news by Tamara Crowe, Ardvreck's Russian matron. It was before tea time on a Sunday afternoon. I had extra cake. I wrote a consoling letter to my mother. "God will look after him". I dreamt many times afterwards that he was still alive. A warder from Stanley prison, a Portuguese from Macao, was with my father when he died. He passed on to my mother in Australia my father's last message.

My grandfather wrote to Ardvreck, taking responsibility for settling the school fees. Ardvreck reduced the fee. Later, when he was late in paying he explained enemy action was the cause. His office had been destroyed. He gave notice that I would be leaving the school at the end of the 1943 summer term.

In a halt in the blitz I went down by train to London to be with my grandparents. The train, crowded with tired soldiers, stopped endlessly. There were barrage balloons overhead as we came close to London. My grandfather took me to Austin Friars in the City to see his office. A bomb had destroyed the front wall. A desk several floors up, hung over the void. That's my desk, he said.

I was sad to leave Ardvreck. In the next term I would have learnt how to fish and how to tie a fly. My parents had planned that I would go on to Glenalmond, a Perthshire school my father had always admired. This was no longer possible.

My mother in the meantime had decided that, one way or another, she would get back to Britain, to be with her parents, getting old, and to see me, her eldest son.

From Sydney my mother and the children had moved to Glen Innes in New South Wales. Colin came top of his class in the local school, jointly with a Chinese girl, thus adding to his accumulating worldwide qualifications.

My mother managed to secure a passage from Sydney to Liverpool aboard the KPM (Royal Dutch Steamship Company) Willem Ruys. This was a speedy modern liner. It left Sydney Harbour the day after the harbour was penetrated by Japanese midget submarines. It sailed alone, and not in convoy, across the Pacific, through the Panama Canal and across the Atlantic. The voyage was fraught. There was constant anti-aircraft and lifeboat practice. The ship stopped frequently to pick up survivors from their life-rafts. Japanese submarines waited for ships passing through the Panama Canal, and German submarines lay in wait on the other side. One of the children was ill. There was the nightmare thought that the ship might be torpedoed in mid Pacific.

They arrived safely in Liverpool. I met them finally at Bridge of Dun, a little country station just to the west of Montrose. My mother was plumper than I remember. I met my little sister Hilary for the first time. My two little brothers came with unfamiliar Australian accents and convincing renderings of the Australian national anthem – "Australia's sons let us rejoice, for we are young and free…"

We stayed for a time in Panmure Cottage, my grandmother's house, and the home of my father, my uncles and my aunt Bessie. While we were there my mother received a letter from Lord Elton, chairman of the Rhodes Trust, a trust created in accordance with the will of Cecil Rhodes in furtherance of the aims of the Empire.The letter said that the Trust wished to help in some way those who had suffered in Hong Kong. They had consulted the head of the National Insurance Company of Canton and he had given them my mother's name as widow of Henry Russell Forsyth, who had given his life for the Empire. The Trust offered my mother a place at Christ's Hospital, free of all cost for the years of her son's education. My mother knew nothing of Christ's Hospital, a City of London school founded in 1553 as the last act of Edward VI, son of Henry VIII and Jane Seymour. Its foundation followed the closure of the monastic schools when Henry split from Rome. My place at Christ's Hospital was in the giving of "Geoffrey Dawson, Editor of The Times."

My mother after consideration (it meant I would go to school in Sussex when she knew my father would have liked me to be brought up in Scotland) accepted the Trust's offer.

I went to school there in September of 1943.

Letter from B.A. Proulx to Mrs M.H. Forsyth, Mitherie Heughfield, Bridge of Earn

59 Cagood Street, Ottawa, Canada
August 11th 1942

Dear Mrs Forsyth

I have received a letter from Mrs Robb, and she has sent me your letter also.

I knew your son Russell well, knew him for years, in Hong Kong. When the full story of the Battle of Hong Kong comes out later, I can assure you that you will be more proud of him. I say "more" because I know you must be very proud of him now. It is the opinion of everyone who fought that "Rusty" will be decorated posthumously. I know whereof I speak, believe me.

No doubt you know he was in command of the Hong Kong Scottish, the best Company in the Hong Kong Volunteer Defence Force. I saw Russell and Mr Prophet the night before the big battle below Stanley Fort. That was on the night of Dec 22nd around 9 p.m. I had gone over to personally thank Prophet and his detachment of the Scottish for the fine job they performed on the night previous in facing and cleaning up a Jap patrol which barred our passage from the besieged Repulse Bay Hotel. They told me they expected a big fight the following day and it was in this fight that Russell was killed. Prophet managed to get away by jumping into the sea and swimming a few miles to the end of Stanley Peninsular. They say that Prophet will also be decorated – I think so personally and I hope this comes about.

The Hong Kong Defence Force covered itself in glory and suffered heavy casualties. They were second to none - as their crest reads. I am proud to have been a part of that force, a force which included such grand old gentlemen as Rogers, Pearce, Des Voeux, men in their seventies and who died in the front line defending their homes.

I wish to tender to you and to Russell's family in Australia my deepest sympathy. Your letter showed me you have a lot of courage, such courage as only British women have.

Sincerely yours

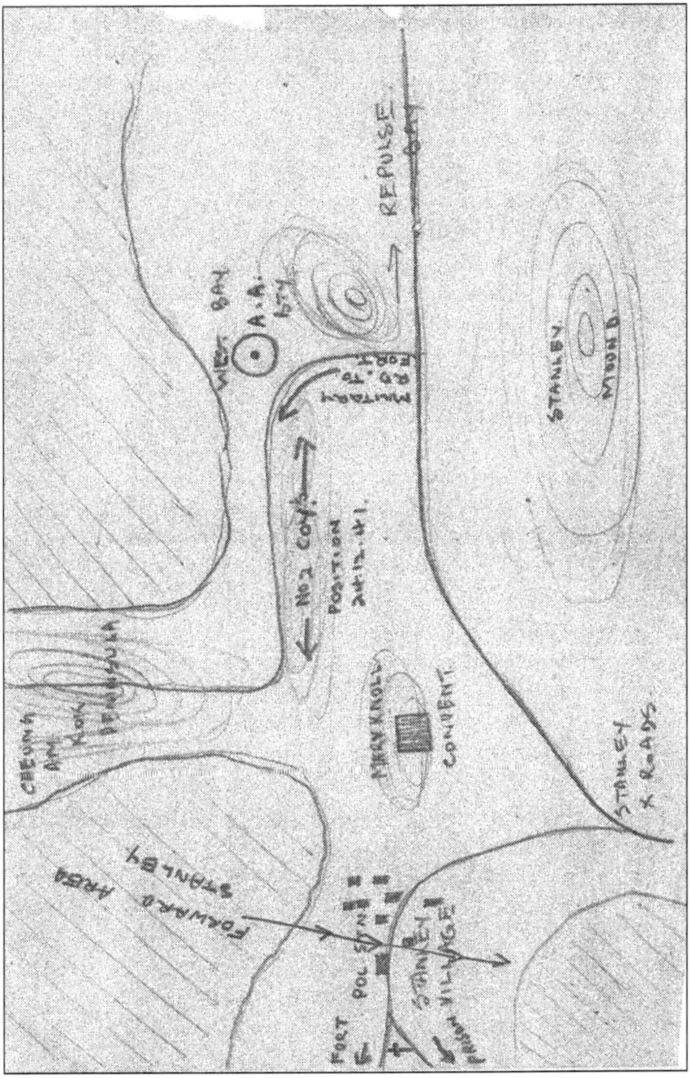

The Battlefield at Stanley

Letter from Captain Prophet 18.10.45

27 Hillcrest Road, Dundee 17th October

Post mark 18 Oct 1945

To Mrs Elaine Forsyth,

2 Braid Farm Road, Edinburgh 10

My dear Elaine,

Arrived home yesterday after a splendid ten day's trip by sea.

It is impossible my dear to convey to you how I feel about your loss of Rusty.

From the time I was a nipper going to school, when I felt so proud to have the privilege of carrying his bag to the rugger field, he was my hero. In later life when I arrived in Hong Kong he was both a father and brother to me and I always knew I had his broad shoulders to lean on in times of trouble.

During the days of the war in Hong Kong we had grown into close friendship and I shall never forget the night when I saw him last in Stanley on the 24th December he felt he was sending his company out to their doom while he was remaining behind in comparative safety and one could see he did not like it. Little did we appreciate what the end would be, that he would go and that we should survive.

The fight that was put up by Rusty in command of the forward area at Stanley when the Japanese launched their final attack on Xmas Eve, is a tale of courage and gallantry which could never be surpassed and it is without due to his efforts that the garrison at Stanley was saved from slaughter. The Japanese attack was held up there for five hours by Rusty and a mere handful of men against thousands and even up to the last he was directing the attack and refused to be moved out of the battle area. No decoration could be high enough for the show that was put up but that my dear is no recompense for the loss of Rusty.

I shall always remember him as a man who was the essence of man and stood out head and shoulders above all others in every phase of life.

It seems mere empty words to offer you my sincerest sympathy but I do so now.

Helen and I will be through to see you very soon and then I can give you the story in more detail. I have Rusty's glengarry which I picked up in Stanley after the surrender along with a photograph of Alastair. I shall bring them to you.

God bless you my dear.

Letter from Colonel H.R.Rose

8 Carew Road, Wallington, Surrey

To Mrs M.E, Forsyth, 2 Braid Farm Road, Edinburgh 10

Postmark 11 Feb 1946

I am afraid this is a vert belated letter but I have only just got your address from the Colonial Office.

I was most terribly sorry about Rusty's death. I expect you have already heard from others what a magnificent show he put up in the defence of Stanley .

I was not on the Stanley side of the Island myself but from the accounts of those who were present your husband's efforts to stop the main Japanese attack on Stanley were absolutely heroic and his personal gallantry can never be forgotten.

The whole of the HKVDC did extremely well but Rusty's gallant stand was truly magnificent and I have never heard of a finer example of self-sacrifice and devotion to duty. His stand at Stanley was the most gallant act in the whole defence of Hong Kong.

I do hope you and your family are all right. I think the last time I saw you was at a picnic lunch on the way to Fanling –and that's a long time ago – now I suppose the family is fast growing up.

If there is anything I can do please let me know or anything you would like me to find out. Although this is so long after I do offer you my deepest sympathy.

Yours sincerely,

H.R.Rose

A dubious account – what is Tim Carew's source?

THE SUNDAY EXPRESS NOVEMBER 20 1960

The DAY HONG KONG FELL

THIS WAS CHRISTMAS DAY FOR A DEFEATED GARRISON

Surrender...the Japs spit on the British

PRIVATE WALTER STUTZ was the sort of soldier who dropped his rifle during a ceremonial parade; who caused sergeant-majors to clench their fists and gaze to the sky; whose involuntary clashes with authority were always good for a laugh in the barrack room. But no man in the Middlesex Regiment laughed at Private Stutz after December 23, 1941.

It was, of course, entirely his own fault he was wounded during the last stages of the battle for Hongkong.

by TIM CAREW

SIR MARK YOUNG
A bitter duty: to surrender Hongkong to the Japs.

For him, the hopeless battle is over
Ahead lie the years of captivity

THE PIPER

THE MATRON

WHISPER

SILENCE . . .

COMFORTERS

At last it seemed that the Japs had tired of hacking wounded men to death, and were in need of more subtle diversions. Their eyes alighted on the nurses.

© TIM CAREW, 1960

THE END

Sunday Express Nov 1960

HONGKONG letter.

"B.A.Proulx of the American Volunteer Group, wrote from Calcutta on April the 10th. — Dorothy Coates'husband was alive and safe, but held at North Point Japanese military prison. Mr.Proulx escaped the night of January 27th and got away to Calcutta by walking, paddling, and motor trucks, covering 3500 miles through Waichow, Kukong and Kweiyang in 59 days.

"Of "Tiny" Coates Mr Proulx said., — He is honestly well and cheerful as ever. I went through the war with him and believe me did some good work all over the shop, no fooling. Was on the same watch with him at Lamma and we ended up in the mountains with rifles, fighting like hill-billies, especially good ones too. "Tiny" was away from me for a few days around Stanley where he put in good work under Forsythe who was killed, then he came back to us. We were seven of us who stuck together in prison, first at "Shamshuipo, then at North Point where we were transferred on Jan.24th. The seven in our group were Tiny, Jupp, Harrison, Westwood, self, Worrall and Evans of the B.A.T... Tell Mrs.Irene Evans that her husband is O.K. (Bill Evans wife is Beryl,George's first cousin:both Parents in Shanghai with Beryl's in-laws)

I can't remember the names of all of them, but some killed are Gregory, Dulley (of Jardines), Tam Pearce, George Tinson, Rogers, the American Exchange broker, Des Voeux, the broker, Viner Gordon Fidding, Forsythe, Mackinley and Winter-Blithe from Deacons, Johnny Hearn the jockey, and there are a great many more.

Of the B.A.T. the men I saw, O'Grady, Sullivan, Merritt, one other whose name I cannot remember, are O.K. Merritt is in civilian camp and is being expatriated. I got away, taking two Dutch submarine Officers, none of the boys in our little mess would come. Between the two camps about 15 have escaped. I saw many of the homes on my way crawling through Hongkong to Shekko and they are in a mess, looted, etc. Peak Mansions where you had your flat was badly shelled and the flats are all looted. We all lost our personal belongings.

-x-x-x-x-x-x-x-x-x-

Benny Proulx escapes Jan 1942

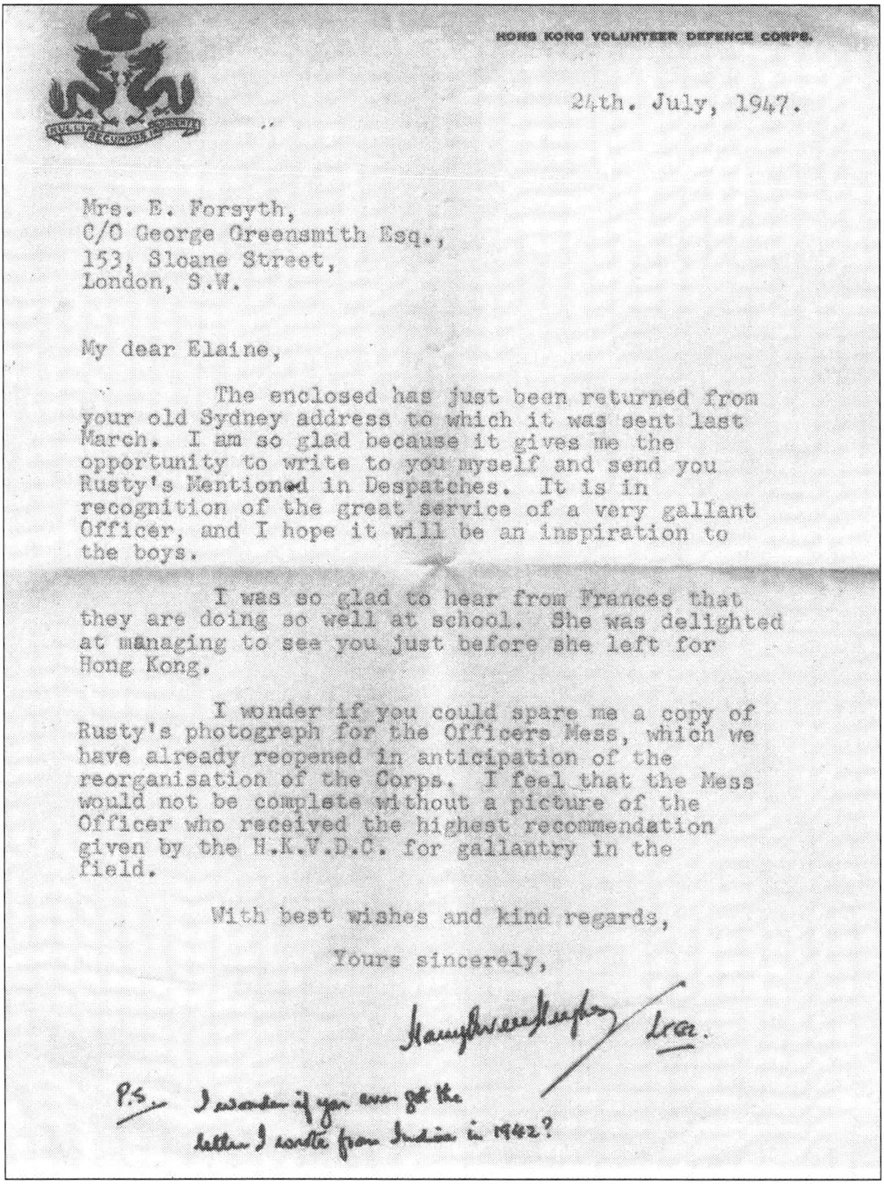

HONG KONG VOLUNTEER DEFENCE CORPS.

24th. July, 1947.

Mrs. E. Forsyth,
C/O George Greensmith Esq.,
153, Sloane Street,
London, S.W.

My dear Elaine,

The enclosed has just been returned from your old Sydney address to which it was sent last March. I am so glad because it gives me the opportunity to write to you myself and send you Rusty's Mentioned in Despatches. It is in recognition of the great service of a very gallant Officer, and I hope it will be an inspiration to the boys.

I was so glad to hear from Frances that they are doing so well at school. She was delighted at managing to see you just before she left for Hong Kong.

I wonder if you could spare me a copy of Rusty's photograph for the Officers Mess, which we have already reopened in anticipation of the reorganisation of the Corps. I feel that the Mess would not be complete without a picture of the Officer who received the highest recommendation given by the H.K.V.D.C. for gallantry in the field.

With best wishes and kind regards,

Yours sincerely,

Harry Owen Hughes Lt.Col.

P.S. I wonder if you ever got the letter I wrote from India in 1942?

Panmure Cottage,
MONTROSE,
Angus, Scotland.

8.

Dear Mr. Smythe,

My Father has written to me to say that through some influential friends of his in London there is a reasonable probability of securing an assignment of a Rhodes Scholarship for Christ's Hospital, Horsham. My Father thinks that in my circumstances it is an opportunity which should be taken advantage of if, in fact, it can be secured.

I know how sorry you would feel if I withdrew Alastair, but in my Father's opinion he is the most desirable candidate to put forward. Colin, my second boy, has not yet reached the age limit, which is between 9 and 11, and, furthermore, I doubt whether, in the circumstances, he would be able to pass the necessary entrance examination.

The suggestion rather upsets the ideas I have recently held, and I should very much appreciate receiving any views you may have upon the matter.

Thanking you in anticipation, and with kind regards, believe me,

Yours sincerely,

D. Smythe, Esq.,
Ardvreck,
Crieff,
Scotland.

10

1942 – After Australia

My mother, my two brothers and sister, returned from Australia to Britain in 1942, in the middle of the war.

We had no money. We stayed for a time in Panmure Cottage, my Scottish grandmother's house in Montrose. We moved from there to an unattractive flat in Edinburgh, in Arden Street. There were skirmishes, gang battles, with other children in the block. We soon after moved out from the centre to the south side of the city, to no. 2 Braid Farm Road. This was a bungalow with a little garden, across the road from the Braid Hills Hotel, a Victorian pile built in the 1880s and now part of the Best Western group.

As newcomers we children were again embroiled in gang warfare. There were no guns, drugs or knives, just hostilities which sometimes degenerated from shouting insults into fights. The Braids in genteel Morningside at least gave my mother less cause for concern, although gang warfare in a milder form persisted.

I am not sure how she was able to buy the house. My parents may have had a little capital outside Hong Kong, including the remnants of the £4,000 George Greensmith gave his daughter when she married. The Edinburgh house cost £2,000. We sold it by sealed bids a few years later for £6,100. The other two bids were £4,000 or a little more. The last of the three bidders was desperate to find a home for his mother-in-law.

My mother's income, as a major's widow was £7 per week. George Greensmith no doubt helped out. There were a number of Hong Kong families who had settled in Edinburgh or nearby – one reason why we moved to Edinburgh. They understood the situation, everything was rationed, there was nothing in the shops. These neighbours were generously supportive, giving all sorts of things we couldn't find or buy.

My Uncle Allan contributed an Afshar rug he had bought for 5 guineas when he was in Persia with the South Persian Rifles. We have it still.

A sadder story is the tale of our Hong Kong silver. In the chaos that followed the Christmas Day surrender of the colony Doctor Durran stopped a Chinese up on the Peak with a sack on his back. In it was the silver from our house. He took the sack and entrusted it to his amah. The Chinese in Hong Kong suffered terribly during the Japanese occupation. There was very little food. But the amah kept the silver. When the British returned, Dr Durran collected the silver from the amah, and rang my mother in Edinburgh with the good news. He fixed a day when he would bring it to her from his home in Perth. He turned up in Edinburgh distraught. The silver had been stolen at Perth station.

For the next few years our home was at Braid Farm Road. I was at school in Sussex. I left Ardvreck in the summer of 1943. Lord Elton, Chairman of the Rhodes Trust, had written (30.9.1942) in the name of the Rhodes Trustees to my mother offering a place for me at Christ's Hospital in Sussex. This was in recognition of my father's "distinguished service to the Empire". Arthur Morse, head of the Hong Kong Shanghai Bank, had helped to arrange this. Geoffrey Dawson, former editor of The Times, had a presentation to Christs Hospital and he signed the formal application for a place for me. Elaine's father advised her to accept the offer, to be educated free of all charge. "It is sufficiently tempting for you to abandon the hope of having them all educated in Scotland". It was an agonising decision for my mother as she knew what Rusty's wish had been. My grandmother took me to Victoria station in September 1943 and we took the train to Christ's Hospital (it had its own station) to begin my first term there.

Our home however was still in Edinburgh and at the beginning and end of each term, until we moved, I took the long train journey between Edinburgh and Sussex. At the beginning of each term my grandmother would meet me at King's Cross when I arrived from Edinburgh and we would take a cab to the flat in Sloane Street. Next day Kathleen the maid would bring me breakfast at the place laid for me. She would wear an apron and cap and celluloid cuffs. My grandfather sat opposite, with The Times on a silver stand in front of him. When he left for the City he would wish me well and press a note into my hand.Later I would walk with my grandmother to Victoria Station where the train for Christ's Hospital would be waiting. On that first day my grandmother and I were in the same compartment as John Purkis and his mother. John and I were in the same house at school, we went to Oxford at the same time and we have been in touch ever since - not least as joint founders of the Barchester Club, a select few who celebrate Trollope, dedicated to his memory as novelist and inventor of the letter box.

Brother Colin was at school with George Watson's academy in Edinburgh, and later, with his brother Murray at Hurst Grange, an ill-fated prep school in Stirling. After Colin and Murray had left, the one-armed headmaster, Mr Pope, went to prison for the usual disgraceful reasons.

From Edinburgh I went on a number of cycling trips. With my cousin Sandy, a few weeks older than me, I went youth-hostelling in the Scottish Borders, also on the east coast of Scotland, where we fortuitously met up with Frances Mary Allan, another cousin, and her sister. With Graham Anderson, a schoolmate, we cycled up to the Trossachs. With others from school, including one of the staff, the cross-eyed Mr Styles, we cycled up to the north coast of Scotland, staying at our northern most point at the youth hostel in Tongue. I rode down the steep hill into Tongue, in driving rain, on the back seat of Mr Styles' tandem. He was virtually blinded by the rain on his glasses, increasing the thrill. We swam in the sea, the water was chokingly cold.

My longest cycling journey was from Edinbugh all the way south to school in Sussex. The family waved me off from our Edinburgh home but I had to return almost at once, from the end of the road, with a puncture. On the journey south I stayed at youth hostels, the first, if I remember rightly, at Otterburn; later at Grantham, having to my eternal shame, taken a lift on a lorry via the ICI works at Billingham. Next stop was Castle Hedingham in Essex, then across the river and on to Kemsing, where I called in on my parents' friends Eric (ex Volunteer) and Mary Bryden and John Masters, Mary's brother. John was a casualty of war. He gave up his job to look after his Kentish smallholding and his pigs. At the hostel there was a ferociously Socialist lady who swore if given the chance she would assassinate prime minister Clement Attlee, as a traitor to the Socialist cause. Onwards it was a leisurely ride back to school, at Horsham.

My mother had the beginnings of a sentimental relationship with a doctor who lived close by in Edinburgh. Doctor Lothian? It might have come to something; but the doctor was a bachelor, a veteran of the war in the desert. Marriage with a widow with four children was not part of his life plan. Nor do I think my mother seriously contemplated, after Rusty, another marital commitment.

My mother took me to see "Brief Encounter" at a Princes Street cinema, about a doctor and a married woman who met by chance at a railway station. It saddened her. I as a teenager who knew little of life was not an adequate confidante.

Edinburgh was cold. (The Brylcreem froze in the bedroom I shared with my brother). My sister Hilary had constant ear trouble. There were some loyal friends but it was far from my mother's parents, now getting old, and her English homeland. She decided to move South. We bought Downlands Cottage on the Pilgims Way in Kemsing in Kent.

I met my mother at the nearest railway station, Otford. She was to show me the new house. Also at the station was Molly Bennett, an exuberant Australian neighbour my mother had already met. She was there to meet her daughter Susan, an unrequited love of mine for years to come. She married a writer on the arts, a specialist on Paul Nash. She learnt Russian and was translating a novel when last year, stepping off the pavement in Oxford Street she was struck down by a bus.

The neighbours who had encouraged us to come to Kent were the Brydens. Eric Bryden was a Captain with my father in the Scottish Company of the Volunteers. He was captured at Stanley after the fight. For the years of the war he was a prisoner of the Japanese. He used to be a plump, cheerful gin drinker. He came back gaunt, but revived. Mary, his wife, my Aunt Mary, and their two young daughters, Betty and June, were with my mother in Australia.

In Kemsing Eric, as my father's long time friend did his best to teach me the first principles of accounting. He had joined Dodwells, a China trader, and I used to envy him his worldwide travels. He preferred to be at home. Some time after my mother died, he fell dead on the way to his bath.

In 1950 I went abroad for the first time on my own, but with my cousin Sandy. We took the boat from Newcastle. The open sea was rough. It was still a time of food rationing in England. About ten of us sat down at a round table, loaded with good things to eat. Only two of us finished the meal – myself and a little redheaded gnome of a gardener from Norway. Keep eating he said. It was good advice.

I left school at the end of the 1951 summer term. In my last year I was a Classical Grecian, that is to say, in the classical sixth form, studying Latin and Greek, under the formidable Mr McNutt. He was the Ximenes of the Observer crossword puzzle, so named after one of the most dreaded of the Spanish Inquisitors. As a Grecian I was entitled to wear a Grecian's velvet cuffs on my long blue gown and a silver buckle on my leather girdle.

Also that year I was head of house, with my own study and a coal fire. It was an unexpected promotion. My predecessor in office was expelled. Our housemaster, the elegant Edward Malins, formerly with the Indian cavalry, chose me to replace him. Running the house and keeping discipline was a valuable lesson, never forgotten.

At the start of the year, to my mother's great delight, I won a scholarship to Keble College, Oxford.

On my return from the interview at Oxford I called in at Downlands Cottage, our home in Kemsing. My grandmother Lizzie had finally left London and was living in the house next door. I went to see her and she gave me a bottle of wine, to take back to school. As I left, she called out: "don't forget to warm the claret". They were her last words to me.

I took the bottle back to school, and that evening, after the rest of the house had gone to bed, opened it to share with a few who had remained. We were not supposed to drink. In came Edward Malins, the housemaster. I offered him a glass. He complimented my grandmother on the quality of the claret.

Prior to my interview at Keble I had an earlier unsuccessful round of exams and interviews at Oxford. It was in mid winter. I stayed in ice-cold rooms in Worcester College. At the end of this first attempt I went back by train, rather gloomily, to Kemsing. I found myself in the same compartment as my Uncle Eric Bryden. He said he was very sorry to hear about my grandfather George and was shocked to learn I had not heard the news that he had died. My mother, in case it should disturb me in the middle of my exams had not told me.

My next visit to Oxford ended more successfully. My first interview was at Wadham College. The grand inquisitor this time was the head of college, the redoubtable Sir Maurice Bowra. He sat at the head of the table, with two junior inquisitors in low chairs on either side. I began uncomfortably as I had entered the interview room prematurely and had to withdraw. There was a barrage of questions. One of the junior inquisitors asked if I thought the Romans would have been upset by Aeneas' unmanly habit of breaking into tears. I said I thought heroes with heroic passions were allowed to cry. At the end of the interview there was another awkwardness as I walked by mistake into the broom cupboard.

The Keble interview was more relaxed. There were two dons and two armchairs and one left for me. They asked if I had done National Service or would do it after university. I said I was exempt. Why? they asked. I am deaf in one ear. They leant forward excitedly. Which ear? They asked. The right, I said, perplexed at their keen interest. So are we, they both said – and they had carefully arranged the chairs so that they could hear, but I could not. There was hilarity: and a relaxed interview that I was quite comfortable with. I was awarded an Open Scholarship to Keble. But only after one further interview at St Caths, at Cambridge. The last question was which university would you prefer. My answer must have settled the outcome.

Two years later my brother Colin, having been head of school at Wellington and done National Service with the Rifle Brigade in Kenya during the Mau Mau campaign, followed me, with a history scholarship, to Keble.

Both of us enjoyed our university days enormously, behaved disgracefully, and ended with respectable second class degrees.

My mother and I motored up to Eaton Hall in Cheshire to watch Colin's passing out parade as a commissioned officer. Our father, Rusty, had spent time at Eaton Hall in the First War, when it was a hospital for wounded officers.

I was at Oxford from 1951 to 1955. Colin followed from 1955 to 1958. In 1956 my brother Murray won a scholarship to Balliol. The three Oxford scholarships were a great delight for my mother.

Lord Elton, Rhodes Trust, to Elaine 30.9.1942

(From temporary address Rhodes House, Oxford)

Dear Madam,

The Rhodes Trustees have a presentation to Christ's Hospital in the name of one of their number, Mr Geoffrey Dawson, and are anxious to employ it on behalf of the child of some parent who has rendered distinguished service to the Empire. They have received particulars of your late husband's career and of your son, Alistair, from the Colonial Office. Your husband's record of service is undoubtedly one which would lead the Trustees to wish to help his son, and I am writing to you to ask whether you would wish to have the boy admitted to Christ's Hospital on Mr Geoffrey Dawson's presentation, and, if so, whether you would be good enough to let me have the necessary particulars. You will see from the form which I enclose that the child must be between nine and eleven years of age and that if admitted he may be educated free of all charge. Will you kindly let me know the date of his birth, the total number of children, and full particulars of your gross income. If you wish to have the boy presented and the particulars you send appear to qualify him for presentation, the next step will be for me to obtain the official form from Christ's Hospital for you to fill up and for Mr Dawson subsequently to sign. Your son would then, presumably, appear at the examination either next November or next March,

Yours sincerely,

Elton

(Lord Elton) Secretary

B.9

ALL COMMUNICATIONS TO BE ADDRESSED TO THE SECRETARY.
TELEGRAMS, "AUGURY, LONDON."
TELEPHONE, WHITEHALL 0187.

The Rhodes Trust
Seymour House, Waterloo Place

TEMPORARY ADDRESS,
RHODES HOUSE,
OXFORD.
TEL. 48165.

~~LONDON, S.W.1.~~

30th September 1942.

Dear Madam,

The Rhodes Trustees have a Presentation to Christ's Hospital in the name of one of their number, Mr. Geoffrey Dawson, and are anxious to employ it on behalf of the child of some parent who has rendered distinguished service to the Empire. They have received particulars of your late husband's career and of your son, Alistair, from the Colonial Office. Your husband's record of service is ~~evidently~~ undoubtedly one which would lead the Trustees to wish to help his son, and I am writing to you to ask whether you would wish to have the boy admitted to Christ's Hospital on Mr. Geoffrey Dawson's Presentation, and, if so, whether you would be good enough to let me have the necessary particulars. You will see from the form which I enclose that the child must be between nine and eleven years of age and that if admitted he may be educated free of all charge. Will you kindly let me know the date of his birth, the total number of children, and full particulars of your gross income? If you wish to have the boy presented and the particulars you send appear to qualify him for presentation, the next step will be for me to obtain the official form from Christ's Hospital for you to fill up and for Mr. Dawson' subsequently to sign. Your son would then, presumably, appear at the examination either next November or next March.

Yours sincerely,

(Lord Elton) Secretary.

Mrs. Forsyth
Panmure Cottage
Montrose.

GG/R

8.2

Bourke, Schiff & Co.

Stock & Share Brokers

Partners:
all British Nationality

34. Bishopsgate,

(and Stock Exchange)

London

E.C.2.

3rd September 1942.

My dear Elaine,

Morse phoned this morning to ask me to go and see him. He told me that he had just received a communication from the Colonial Office that they were in a position to grant Presentations under the Rhodes Scholarship Scheme to Orphans who had lost their Fathers in the War, and that they would give preferential consideration to boys from the Far East. They had written to Morse to know whether he had any Candidates he could recommend, and he said your name was, naturally, the first that came into his mind. At this stage neither he, nor I, know what the standard of Education required - for entry, but the age of the boys should be between 9 and 11. I believe that everything is free, and in your circumstances I certainly think you should give the matter very serious thought. The School is an excellent one from every point of view, and, as you probably know, enjoys an excellent reputation. They have fine buildings at Horsham.

My first re-action to the suggestion is whether to arrange to withdraw Alastair at the end of this next term and transfer him to Christ's Hospital (in which case you might consider sending Colin to Ardvreck) or if Colin should take advantage of the offer. I just wonder whether Colin, having, through force of circumstances, had to change his school so many times, would be able to pass the necessary examination for entrance. I certainly think the offer is sufficiently tempting for you to abandon the hope of having them all educated in Scotland.

Morse would like to know what your re-action is to the suggestion, and if you agree he would then get more particulars. He thinks it might be six months before any active steps could be taken.

Tell Mother I saw Shah yesterday afternoon. Physically, he looked quite well and spruce. Probably this was because the Barber had been to him a few hours before - taken off three days' beard and moustache and cut his hair. The Hospital is a large one, very pleasantly situated, and I should think very efficiently run. He is quite comfortable there, but is nervous about the time when he will be able to leave his bed - which may be in two or three weeks' time - whether he will be able to stand and move about. He sent his love to you all, and he was certainly better and more cheerful than I expected to find him.

Yours ever,

Dad.

P.T.O.

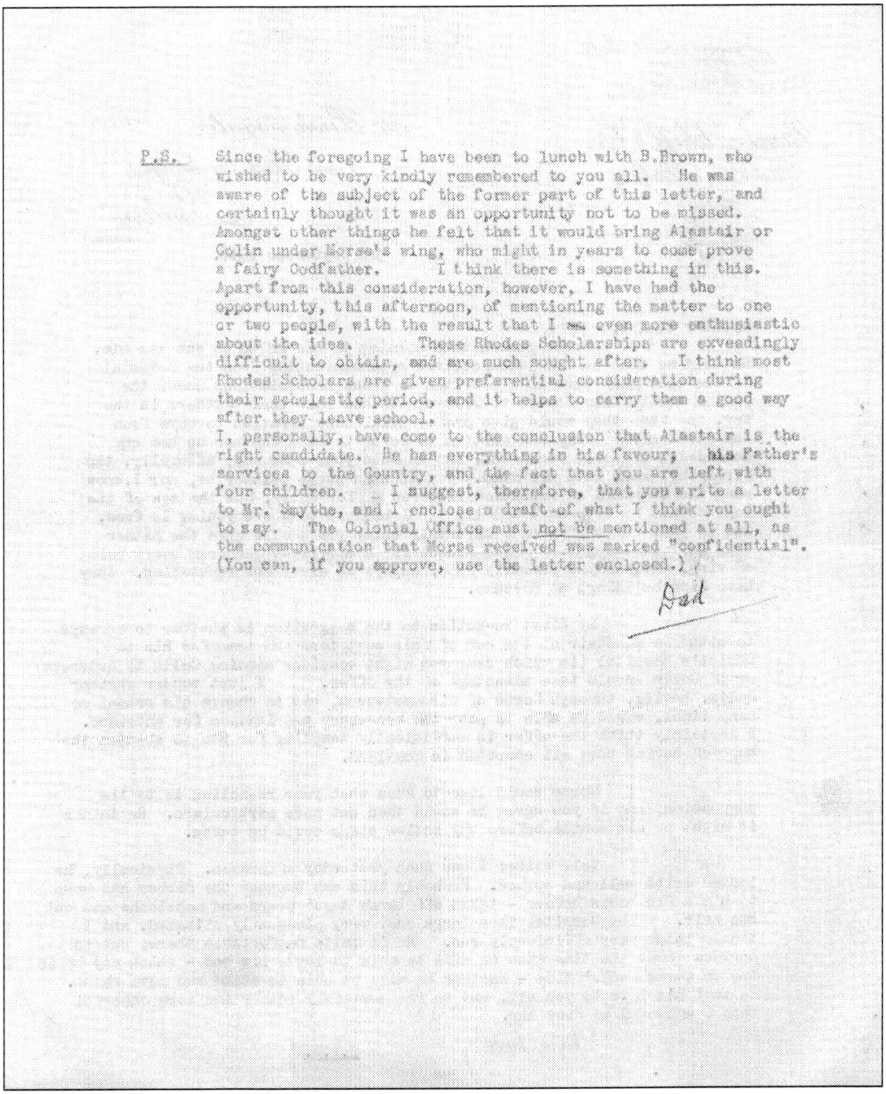

<u>P.S.</u> Since the foregoing I have been to lunch with B.Brown, who wished to be very kindly remembered to you all. He was aware of the subject of the former part of this letter, and certainly thought it was an opportunity not to be missed. Amongst other things he felt that it would bring Alastair or Colin under Morse's wing, who might in years to come prove a fairy Godfather. I think there is something in this. Apart from this consideration, however, I have had the opportunity, this afternoon, of mentioning the matter to one or two people, with the result that I am even more enthusiastic about the idea. These Rhodes Scholarships are exceedingly difficult to obtain, and are much sought after. I think most Rhodes Scholars are given preferential consideration during their scholastic period, and it helps to carry them a good way after they leave school.
I, personally, have come to the conclusion that Alastair is the right candidate. He has everything in his favour; his Father's services to the Country, and the fact that you are left with four children. I suggest, therefore, that you write a letter to Mr. Smythe, and I enclose a draft of what I think you ought to say. The Colonial Office must <u>not be</u> mentioned at all, as the communication that Morse received was marked "confidential". (You can, if you approve, use the letter enclosed.)

Dad

Alastair's Letter to Elaine 9.5.43

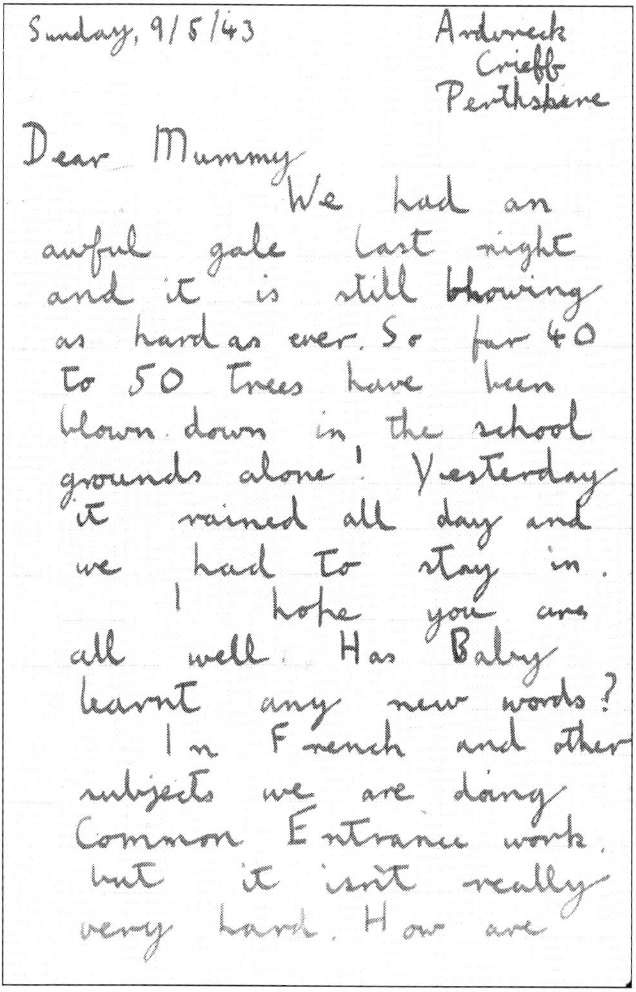

Sunday, 9/5/43

Ardvreck
Crieff
Perthshire

Dear Mummy

We had an awful gale last night and it is still blowing as hard as ever. So far 40 to 50 trees have been blown down in the school grounds alone! Yesterday it rained all day and we had to stay in.

I hope you are all well. Has Baby learnt any new words?

In French and other subjects we are doing Common Entrance work, but it isn't really very hard. How are

Colin and Murray getting on at school? Tell Colin that I have got four ordinary cartridge cases and 12 ~~gold~~ small gold cartridge cases and 2 small silver cartridge cases 18 altogether. Tell Murray that I've still got that rubber he gave me and it is being <u>very</u> useful since it is the only one in the class.

Love from
Alastair

P.S. I have enclosed 3 poems.

Alastair's letter to Elaine from school, 1943

Dear Mummy,

Jerry came over last night real and proper. The alert had just sounded but the danger hadn't. All of sudden there was the crump of bombs, the pop of aeroplane cannons and machine guns and the whoof of A.A. guns. Jerry came diving down firing at a train. After that he went and dropped two bombs. .

Something hit the third bomb while it was still inside the plane and Jerry blew up.

Its been quite cold lately cold enough to keep the milk from going sour. I wore Colin's coat today for the first time. It's lovely and warm.

About the best size of bike would be a 22 or 24 I think.

Have Colin and Baby got better now?

Not much more news this week.

Love from Alastair

Alastair's letter to Elaine 16.7.1944

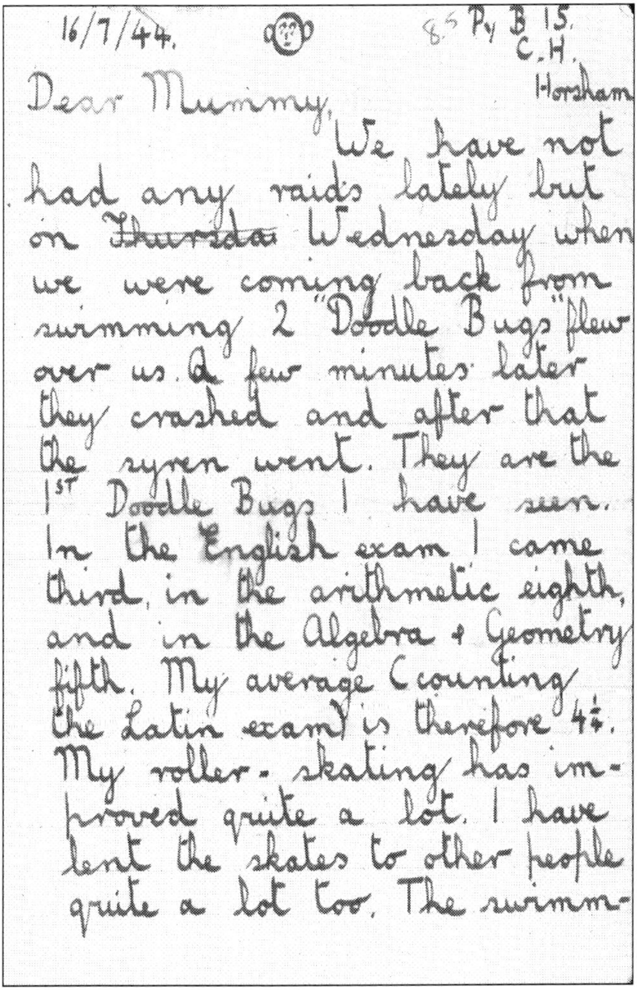
16/7/44. 8.5 Py B 15.
C.H.
Horsham

Dear Mummy,
We have not had any raids lately but on ~~Thursda~~ Wednesday when we were coming back from swimming 2 "Doodle Bugs" flew over us. A few minutes later they crashed and after that the syren went. They are the 1st Doodle Bugs I have seen. In the English exam I came third, in the arithmetic eighth, and in the Algebra + Geometry fifth. My average (counting the Latin exam) is therefore 4¼. My roller-skating has improved quite a lot. I have lent the skates to other people quite a lot too. The swimm-

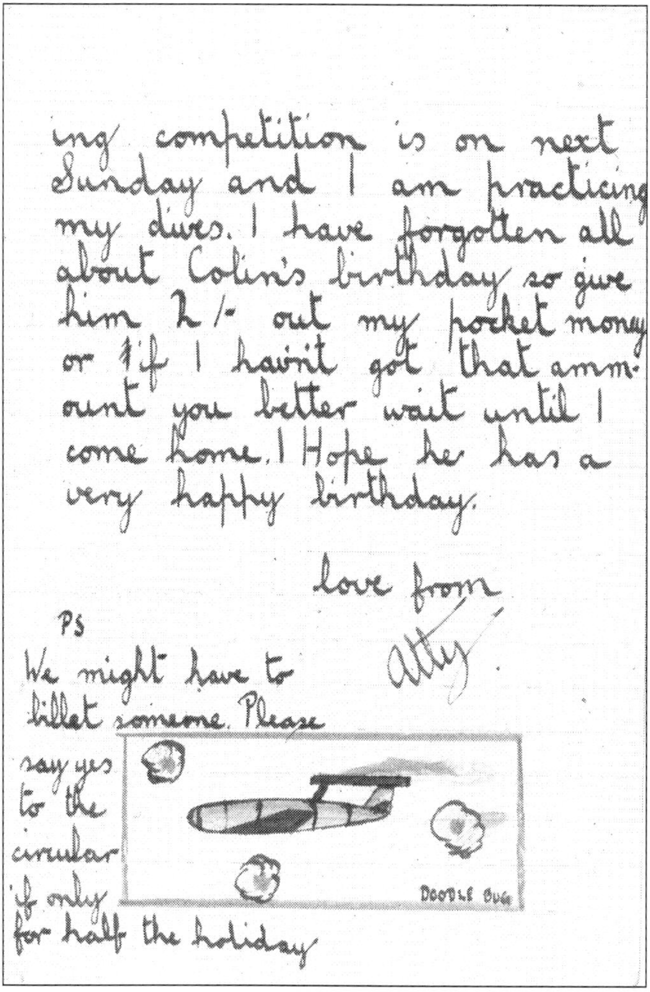

ing competition is on next Sunday and I am practicing my dives. I have forgotten all about Colin's birthday so give him 2/- out my pocket mony or if I havn't got that amm-ount you better wait until I come home. I Hope he has a very happy birthday.

love from

Atty.

PS

We might have to billet someone. Please say yes to the circular if only for half the holiday

Alastair's letter to Elaine 1945

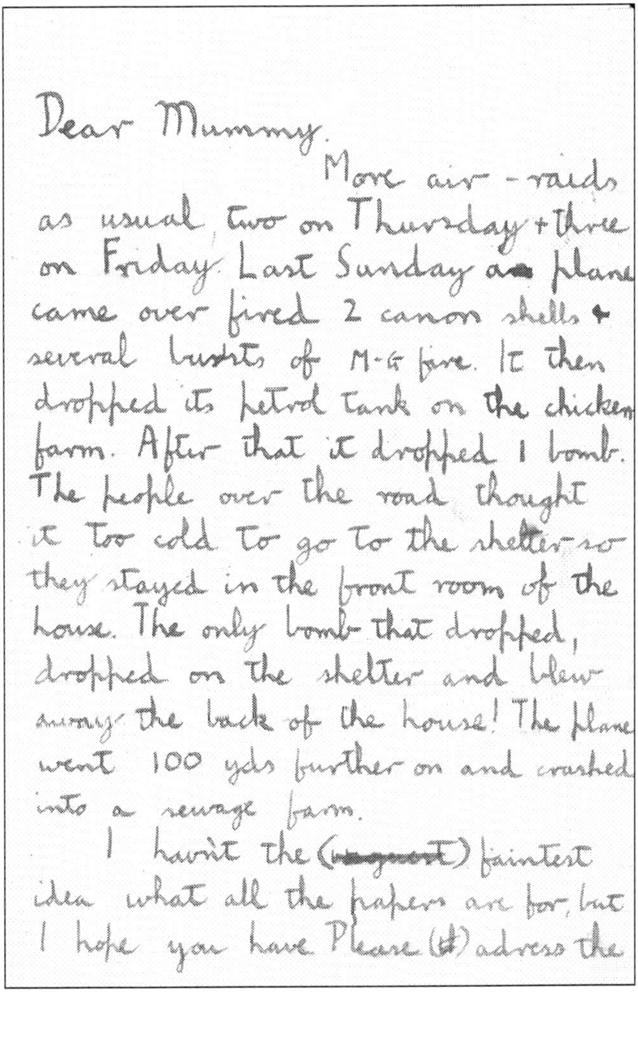

Dear Mummy,

More air-raids as usual, two on Thursday + three on Friday. Last Sunday a ~~[illegible]~~ plane came over fired 2 canon shells + several bursts of M-G fire. It then dropped its petrol tank on the chicken farm. After that it dropped 1 bomb. The people over the road thought it too cold to go to the shelter so they stayed in the front room of the house. The only bomb that dropped, dropped on the shelter and blew away the back of the house! The plane went 100 yds further on and crashed into a sewage farm.

I havn't the (~~[illegible]~~) faintest idea what all the papers are for, but I hope you have. Please (tt) adress the

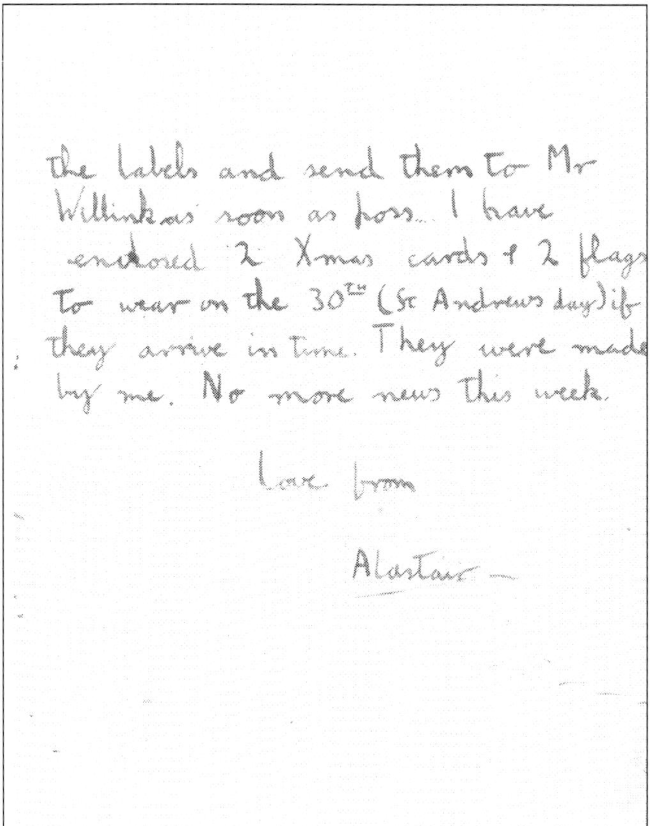
the labels and send them to Mr
Willink as soon as poss.. I have
enclosed 2 Xmas cards & 2 flags
To wear on the 30th (St Andrews day) if
they arrive in time. They were made
by me. No more news this week.

Love from

Alastair

Alastair's letter to Elaine 1945, The end of the War

Dear Mummy,

Didn't the war in Europe end quickly? I never expected it to end so soon. We had a grand time on V.E. day. The news came at 8'o clock on Monday. We all went mad with excitement. We rushed into the quad and began pulling the school bell. Then we got out a styrup pump and began spraying everyone in reach. Eventually we went up to the dormitory where we ragged about for hours. We pushed every mattress off the bed onto the floor, we had pillow fights, and covered the monitors with rugs and sheets. Then Mr Crosland came in and we made our beds again and at some late hour got to sleep.

The next day (Tuesday) we were even worse. Everyone managed to get something red, white and blue to put in their button hole. We charged up to dining hall in a motley rabble making a terrible noise. After breakfast a boy called Allan and I set off on a flag hunt. We went off to the Scout hall as that was the only place we knew that had flags. When we arrived all the doors were locked and all the windows bolted. When we were just about to go away we saw a skylight on the roof open. So we climbed up and discovered it was tied down and we could only get a hand in to cut the cord. There was a drop of about 12 ft but we managed it without any casualties. After looking around for quite a bit we couldn't find a single flag. The store room where most of them were kept was shut but it was a bad lock and we managed to force it open, get a flag and bang it shut again. . Then carrying our one flag triumphantly we made our exit through the window. Soon after we went to the Thanksgiving service. The Chapel was very crowded and we had to sit on a bench in the aisle. Then we went to see a swimming gala down at the pool where they had water polo and life saving etc. One of the best things was when two people had a pillow fight on a pole over the water. At 3 o'clock we all listened to the Prime Minister's speech. At 4.15 (16.15 hrs BDST) there was an open air band concert where they played lots of national anthems and popular songs. After that we went swimming and at 1800 hrs BDST we sat down to a supper of corned beef and roast potatoes, fruit salad and blancmange and coffee. At 9 o'clock we listened to the king's speech and then dressed up in the maddest things to go to the bonfire. This was an old haystack which had been ruined by the rain and boys (!!). On the top of it were placed hundreds of banners, swastikas and effigies of Nazi leaders. Over it all was poured paraffin or something like that and then it was set alight. Right up on a hill as we were we could see all the other bonfires for miles around. At about 11 o'clock we started back and it was long past 24.00 before we were properly asleep.

I havn't much more time so cheerio and I hope you've had as good VE day as I did,

love Atty

PS Received your parcel of pyjamas

11

Epilogue

Anyone who has followed the story this far deserves to know how it continues. This is difficult to do in detail as my own knowledge is limited and subsequent ramifications are prolific. So the story is not complete and many names have been omitted. The reason is not that their achievements are negligible but there is only so much any reader, even if related, can absorb. The intention in what follows is to give an idea of the history of the family in more recent years and its continuing, agreeable complexity.

Firstly, the Greensmiths. There were only two surviving children of my Greensmith grandparents – my mother Elaine, mainly responsible for who I am, and her elder brother, my Uncle Reggie. My mother toiled bravely on to try to take the place of the father her four children had lost, when her eldest was only nine. The strain of it all I am sure led to her early death. She died at fifty five. But not before she had the satisfaction of her three sons winning scholarships to Oxford and her only daughter training to be a doctor at St Thomas's (ultimately to be a consultant psychiatrist).

I ended my time as a director of the merchant bank, J Henry Schroder Wagg.

My brother Colin had a spray of brilliant ideas, including his Panaustralian Unit Trust which for many continuous years out performed the field.

My brother Murray, after history at Balliol, spent a year at the College of Europe in Bruges, taught Politics at Leicester, eventually as Professor, and after leaving Leicester, continued at the Baptist University of Hong Kong. He produced a massive tome on Federalism and more lighthearted works on such subjects as the Abbe Sieyes, an architect of the French Revolution. His Wife, Marie has her own literary output, including well researched intriguing guides to local country house history.

Sister Hilary dedicated her life to the National Health Service and to her son Sholto Kynoch, an organ scholar at Oxford. Hilary and son worked together to develop the Lieder Festival at Oxford, much praised and now (2016) more than ten years old. Sholto's father, James Davidson Kynoch, was a friend of mine at Keble College, Oxford; a lawyer for a few years in London, he left to practice at the criminal bar in Hong Kong, where he died, before his time, leaving a reputation for hard work and honesty.

Reggie's two children were Anne and Jane. Anne married Jack Gerrish., who inherited a clothes factory in East London (he made me a present of my first tweed suit) and a breathtakingly valuable stamp collection.(His father was philatelist to the King). Anne enjoyed life and her four children, one of whom took to horses and another became a Buddhist priest, converting my grandmother's silver lobster forks into bangles for sale by the faithful. Jack, a squash player at Westminster, a young major in the war, met Anne as a WREN (Womens Royal Naval Air Service) in Sri Lanka, They raised a family of four in England, some now in Australia. After sale of the family business he worked for many years for Levi's, makers of jeans.

Jane studied Biology at St Andrews, married a Glaxo chemist and, after he died, took up teaching and became head mistress of a school in Dorset. She has a lively set of talented and devoted grandchildren.

Secondly, the Forsyths. My father's elder brother Allan lived all his life, after the First War, in Bridge of Earn in Perthshire. He was a Church Councillor and Scout Leader and a respected JP. He served in the UK in the second war, towards the end as commandant of a Prisoner of War Camp near Blairgowrie. The toothbrush he brought back on leave was stained brown by the peaty Blairgowrie water.

He married Nan Macdonald, who during the war, in my parents absence, became a dearly loved second mother to me.

They had three sons, my cousins Ian, Sandy and Allan. Ian studied agriculture at Aberdeen and as an entomologist joined the Colonial Office in Ghana. He met and married a fellow entomologist and later, when at RHS Wisley, sold for a song to the Ghanaian Government his masterly work on the diseases of the cocoa plant. Ian and Pamela returned to Belfast, his wife's home town, and both had posts at the University. Ian received an MBE for services to ornithology and late in life produced a definitive work on British bats.

They had two children, Patricia and Elspeth. Patricia is a permanent student. Elspeth is a landscape designer whose husband is employed by the Archaeological Survey of Scotland.

Sandy, Ian's younger brother, only a month older than me and a dear friend, did National service in the Army Catering Corps. They cooked inspirationally in a prolonged attempt to achieve a Royal in front of their regimental name. After the army he joined Macfisheries and rose early in the morning to buy fish at the right price from Grimsby. Soon after, his Aunt Agnes, a distinguished Lady Mayoress of Monmouth and Head Mistress of Monmouth girls' school, funded his first own venture in London, the Bread Basket in Moxon Street, Marylebone. He sold it successfully, returned to Scotland and opened an antique shop near Perth, specializing in Scottish silver (It was said, unjustly, that he had no difficulty in converting an antique spoon into an antique fork to complete an antique set.) He married Pat, a freelance journalist. They had no children but moved to an isolated home in St Martin's by Perth; full of beautiful things, silver, glass and pictures, and two or three enormous dogs. Sandy died of a distressing organ failure, not fully understood, and his wife moved to Majorca, where she enjoys the sun. She was for years a lively and widely read free lance journalist, writing mainly for women, on the secrets of looking good.

Allan, third of the brothers, studied to become a doctor in Edinburgh, joined the RAF and spent much of his National Service as the lone qualified doctor at a remote RAF base in the Andaman Islands. He returned to spend many years as a GP in Perth and part time medical officer at nearby Strathallan School. He married Birgitte, a Swedish physiotherapist he met in Edinburgh. Birgitte learnt "the Gaelic", the only Gaelic speaker in the family, and teaches Yoga for the local authority. On retirement they moved to Drumnakyle, a cottage close to Kinlochrannoch, with dramatic views down Loch Rannoch and across the valley to the great bulk of Schiehallion, lately home to ospreys. They have now sold Drumnakyle, at times unreachable in winter, and moved to more sociable Pitlochry.

Allan and Brigitte have three children, Hector, a technology wizard in Aberdeen, close to the North Sea oilfields, Katarina, a doctor in Edinburgh, married to Austin, an Edinburgh lawyer, and Aileen, married with a family in Perth Australia, A trail of young Swedes used to visit Drumnakyle and young Scots went visiting to Sweden.

My father's only sister was red-headed Bessie, My Auntie Bee. Like all her brothers she went to Montrose Academy and went on from there to a prestigious domestic science college in Edinburgh. She married a rather serious electrical engineer from Manchester (whose family so he claimed gave sixpence to Andrew Carnegie to launch him on his career in the United States). They had two children, my cousins Leslie and Kenneth. Leslie was much like his father but more inclined to joke. He worked for Linotype in Manchester. His wife and adopted daughter survived him. Kenneth went to Hotel School in Glasgow, was an unfailingly witty fellow and married Deirdre, whom he met at the hotel school. With her, unflinchingly Yorkshire, but educated at Dollar Academy in Scotland, of which she is still a governor, they managed together a number of hotels and hostelries, ending at the White Swan at Pickering. This hotel, Deirdre and son Victor, after Kenneth's death out hunting, continue to run, most professionally, as a comfortable market town hotel, with a fine line in Burgundies. There is also a successful daughter, Claire, who lives high up in the clouds of telecommunication with her husband.

All the family members above, linked to Forsyths or Greensmiths, I met, and so can comment on more personally than those who have gone before.

I should add to this list my own six children, in whose hands the future of the kingdom rests – Angus, who for an American company insures vintage cars, Jamie, who transforms houses and sells them, Alexander, a Major in the Queens Royal Hussars, MA War Studies Chenai university, currently assigned to the Canadian Army, John, a specialist in education sector investment in Asia and elsewhere, Arethusa, a Mayfair lawyer advising on tax and trusts, Mary about to start 3 years at the London Academy of Music and Dramatic Art.

Jacki looks after me, as well as indefatigably travelling the world, managing a wide range of corporate and charitable events

So the story, temporarily, ends. I hope the family stays together, and that someone else takes up the tale. But their relatives may object to the long term labour that exiles the prospective author from real life with the rest of them.

Those of them I knew who preceded me were good people, good citizens who contributed in various ways to their communities. If asked to nominate the bounders, among the throng of saints, I would tend to look towards two of them. But both were good company and their true stories were too well kept for me to make anything of them worth reading about.

....

June 2017